To Michael —
Merry Christmas
+ congrats on your
fine reviews.
Phil Donahue

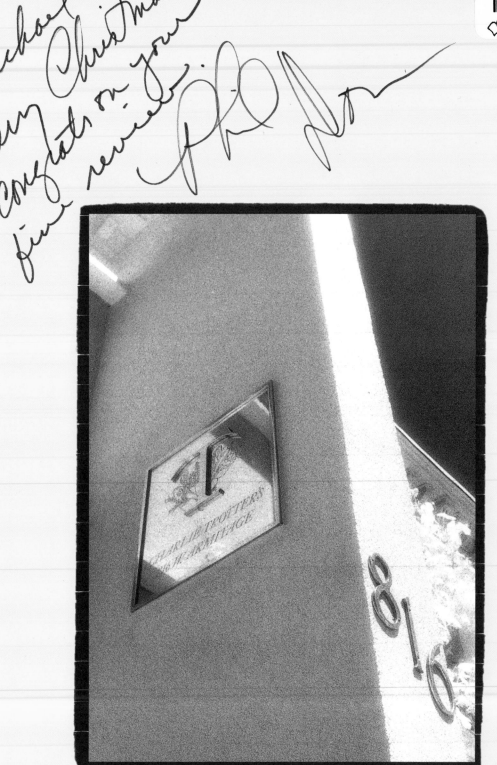

Michael
Congrats on
your reviews!!
Enjoy

Photography Copyright ©1994 Tim Turner, Chicago

Project Coordinator and General Editor, Terry Ann R. Neff, Chicago
Editor, Jackie Wan, Ten Speed Press, Berkeley, California
Recipe Tester, Susie Heller, Cleveland

Published in 1994 by
Ten Speed Press
P.O. Box 7123
Berkeley, California 94707

Library of Congress Cataloging-in-Publication Data

Trotter, Charlie
Charlie Trotter's cookbook / Charlie Trotter
p.   cm.
ISBN 0-89815-628-9

1. Charlie Trotter's (Restaurant) 2. Cookery.
I. Charlie Trotter's (Restaurant) II. Title.
TX714.T77 1994
641.5' 09773'1--dc20   94-29080
CIP

CHARLIE TROTTER'S

Recipes by
Charlie Trotter

Photography by
Tim Turner

Wine Notes by
Joseph Spellman
Renée-Nicole Kubin
Patricia Mowen

Ten Speed Press, Berkeley, California

CONTENTS

I would like to dedicate this book to my mother
and the memory of my late father.

IN APPRECIATION

Dan Burrows

Judi Carle

Geoff Felsenthal

Michael Glass

Steve Greystone

Susie Heller

Adam R. Kallish

Emeril Lagasse

Andrew MacLauchlan

Jennifer Malott

Nelli Maltezos

Mathias Merges

Patricia Mowen

Terry Ann R. Neff

Mitchell Schmieding

Mark Signorio

Joseph Spellman

Larry Stone

Guillermo Tellez

Lynn Trotter

Scott Trotter

Tim Turner

Norman Van Aken

Reginald Watkins

INTRODUCTION

To lose courage is to sin...
work, ever more work, con amore, *therein lies real happiness.*
FYODOR DOSTOYEVSKY

It's all about excellence, or at least working towards excellence. Early on in your approach to cooking—or to running a restaurant—you have to determine whether or not you are willing to commit fully and completely to the idea of *the pursuit of excellence.* I have always looked at it this way: if you strive like crazy for perfection—an all-out assault on total perfection—at the very least you will hit a high level of excellence, and then you might be able to sleep at night. To accomplish something truly significant, excellence has to become a life plan.

When I took my first professional kitchen job, in November 1982, I had no idea where the road would take me. I was hired by Chef Norman Van Aken at Sinclair's Restaurant in Lake Forest, Illinois, and from my first day in the kitchen I knew I had found paradise—cuisine was all I could think about—and it still is! Everything was new and wonderful, and I was fortunate to be exposed to Norman's philosophy on food and cooking. He placed the highest priority on using fresh and seasonal products, and insisted that no shortcuts be taken in any aspect of food preparation. Because I had never worked in a kitchen before, I had nothing with which to compare Norman's approach, but instinctively I knew he was right. His take-the-high-road attitude toward cooking was not only the best way, it was the only way.

Since then, I have worked in several other fine kitchens and I have read literally hundreds of books on cooking technique, food philosophy, and culinary history. I have also traveled around this amazing country and to many parts of Europe. All of these experiences have influenced my approach to cuisine.

When I opened Charlie Trotter's, in August 1987, I tried to bring this knowledge and exposure together into a coherent view on what the modern fine dining experience could be. I thought the blend of European refinement regarding pleasures of the table, American ingenuity and energy in operating a small enterprise, Japanese minimalism and poetic elegance in effecting a sensibility, and a modern approach to incorporating health and dietary concerns would encompass a spectrum of elements through which I could express myself fully. Several years later, I find I am more devoted than ever to this approach.

When it comes to the cuisine itself, I can pass on one thing that I know for sure: ingredients are everything! More important than profound culinary ideas or masterful technique is the commitment to using only the best possible ingredients. Not necessarily luxury products, but foodstuffs at the height of their flavor: potatoes just out of the ground, berries right off the bush, line-caught fish straight from the sea. If you start with the finest, freshest, purest-tasting ingredients, it is genuinely hard to go wrong. Sophisticated cooking techniques and creativity are bonuses, but the foundation of truly fine cuisine is rooted in the foodstuffs themselves.

Cuisine is only about making foods taste the way they are supposed to taste. That may seem obvious, but it really is not. Had he written about food, the eighteenth-century British philosopher Jeremy Bentham might have dismissed some of today's cuisine as *nonsense upon stilts,* and I think he would have been right. Chefs today have so many foodstuffs and culinary ideas at their fingertips that in order to gain complete credibility, precision and control must be evident in their work. For me, purity is the only true approach.

Wines are an integral part of the dining experience at Charlie Trotter's. The idea of pairing foodstuffs with a variety of different wines is one of the most creative aspects of the restaurant. Depending on how it has been prepared, tuna might best be served with a Champagne or Sancerre, or something fuller, such as a Merlot or red Burgundy. In addition, there may be three or four appropriate wines for a single dish. One of the intriguing things about pairing food and wine is that the solutions are often unexpected and exciting. In the end, it comes down to whatever you like to drink; our wine suggestions serve merely as a guide.

No restaurant can run successfully without teamwork. Each member of the team has a role to play, and must play it well, or there can be no ultimate victory. As the leader, I take total responsibility for what is served at Charlie Trotter's; therefore, it is up to me to set the game plan—to articulate my vision, to guide, inspire, and keep the team focused, and at all times, to maintain the goal of excellence. Within this framework, I encourage spontaneity and welcome the contributions of each member of the team. Together we can reach even higher.

In the fall of 1982, I read the following words by the German poet Johann Wolfgang von Goethe, and they have remained my principal inspiration:

Until there is commitment, there is hesitancy, the chance to draw back, always ineffectiveness. Concerning all acts of initiative (and creation), there is one elementary truth, the ignorance of which kills countless ideas and splendid plans: that the moment one definitely commits oneself, then providence moves too. All sorts of things occur to help one that would never otherwise have occurred. A whole stream of events issues forth from the decision, raising in one's favor all manner of unforeseen incidents and meetings and material assistance which no man could have dreamed would have come his way. Whatever you can do or dream you can, begin it. Boldness has genius, power, and magic in it. Begin it now!

The recipes in this book are only a guide. You can use any or all of a recipe, deviate wherever you like, or indeed, substitute ingredients completely if it suits your desires. In fact, you may want to forget about the recipe specifics and use the photographs alone as your inspiration for putting together a meal. You can contemplate food on an intellectual level, but ultimately it is a sensuous experience and it is perhaps best to enjoy it that way.

Charlie Trotter

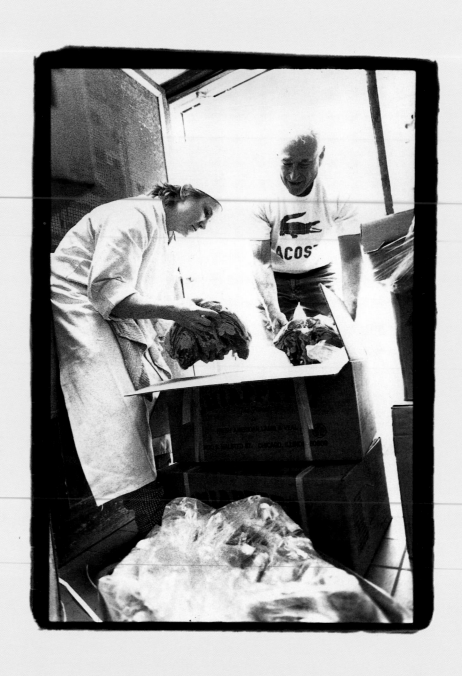

TOMATOES

Tomatoes are my favorite vegetable, but only in season, when they are so sweet and juicy that they can almost quench your thirst as you eat them. I buy organically grown, vine-ripened tomatoes almost exclusively from the Angelic Organic Farm in Caledonia, Illinois. They supply me with tomatoes in all sizes and shapes and in a variety of flavors and colors — yellow, green, purple, even white. They also provide me with many varieties of *heirloom* tomatoes, types that had been abandoned for years because they were not suitable for large-scale production, but that are now being grown for the specialty market. Almost all of them seem to have an unusual sweetness.

Because there are so many different kinds available, tomatoes lend themselves to spontaneous, creative handling. Raw, they can be cut up for a salsa-type preparation to accompany seafood, or they can be tossed with other vegetables in a little olive oil for a salad. They can be roasted whole, then hollowed out and filled with grains or vegetables. They can be layered into a terrine, or even poached in olive oil or duck fat to make a confit that will melt in your mouth with an unbelievable richness. Furthermore, the very essence of the tomato — its water — is one my basic cooking ingredients. I use it in the construction of a wide variety of dishes and sauces. I even braise seafood in it. In fact, tomatoes are so versatile that in August and September, I even feature an all-tomato menu at the restaurant that is invariably a huge hit.

There is a certain misconception that tomato dishes cannot be successfully paired with wine. However, depending on the recipe, they can be nicely matched with a number of wines, both red and white. The heirloom tomatoes in particular are so low in acid that they literally present no problem.

Olive Oil-Poached Tomatoes with Sweet Peas, Veal Stock Reduction, and Red Wine Reduction

In the Midwest, the beginning of tomato season coincides with the end of the season for sweet peas, so this dish is sort of a hello and a good-by to two of my favorite vegetables. It features tomatoes that have been poached in olive oil at a very low temperature for 10 hours or longer, with a result that is hard to put into words. The sweet peas and their juice beautifully augment the already sweet tomatoes, and with the reduction sauces result in a dish of incredible complexity. Ultimately, though, the success of this preparation lies in the simple yet profound harmony of flavors.

Serves 4

8 to 12 vine-ripened Italian plum tomatoes

About 2 cups olive oil

¼ cup sweet peas, shelled

Pea Sauce (recipe follows)

Red Wine Reduction (see Appendix)

Veal Stock Reduction (see Appendix)

Tomato Coulis (see Appendix)

Salt and pepper to taste

Tarragon sprigs

METHOD Cut off the very top of the tomatoes. Place in a small roasting pan and add enough olive oil to just cover. Cover the pan with a lid or aluminum foil and place in a 175-degree oven for 10 to 12 hours (this can be done overnight). Remove from the oven and cool at room temperature. Carefully remove the tomatoes from the oil and peel. Using a thin, narrow knife and approaching from the cut side, carefully remove as many of the seeds as possible. (The oil can be saved for poaching tomatoes again or for use in vinaigrettes. Refrigerate the oil, which will cause it to separate from any tomato juices that may have seeped out as the tomatoes were poaching. These juices are delicious over poached fish.)

Just before serving, warm the tomatoes in the oven and season lightly with salt and pepper. Blanch the peas in boiling, salted water. Strain and lightly season with salt and pepper.

ASSEMBLY Place a mound of peas on the center of each plate. Spoon some Pea Sauce on the peas, and place 2 or 3 tomatoes on each mound. Drizzle some warm Red Wine Reduction, Tomato Coulis, and Veal Stock Reduction onto each plate. Garnish with fresh tarragon.

Pea Sauce

¼ cup chopped shells from sweet peas

¼ cup sweet peas

½ cup Sweet Corn Broth (see Appendix)

2 tablespoons Herb Oil (see Appendix)

2 tablespoons grapeseed oil

3 tablespoons Parsley Juice (see Appendix)

METHOD Blanch the shells in boiling, salted water for 5 minutes, then shock them in ice water. Place the shells in a blender and pour in enough Sweet Corn Broth to cover (about ¼ cup). Blend for 2 to 3 minutes and pass through a fine mesh strainer. Blanch the peas in boiling, salted water for 1 minute or so, then shock in ice water. Place the peas in the blender and add the remaining corn broth. Blend until smooth. Add the juice from the shells to the blender along with the Herb Oil, grapeseed oil, and Parsley Juice. Blend on high speed for 45 seconds to 1 minute. Season with salt and pepper. Any leftover sauce can be used for baby food or to make a delicious soup.

Wine Notes

The key to this light, slightly sweet preparation is its seasonality; only in midsummer will plum tomatoes be deliciously ripe enough and peas still young and sweet enough to make the dish satisfying. This is also true of a number of fine American Sauvignon Blancs that are released in the spring and summer following last fall's harvest. On release, they are vibrantly fruity, with a sassy herbal edge, and give wonderful refreshment. This is especially true of those wines that see little or no oak. And a good Sauvignon's acidity will certainly support the dish. Our favorite examples are from Spottswoode, Quivera, and Frog's Leap.

Pyramid of Tomatoes, Roasted Poblanos, Black Beans, Avocado, and Tomatillos with Black-Eyed Peas, and Coriander Juice

Not only is this dish spectacular from a visual standpoint, it is also very hearty and refreshing.
In it, the pure, clean flavor of vine-ripened tomatoes is given a lift by the very powerful but delicate
Coriander Juice, while the black beans and black-eyed peas provide the necessary substance.
If you are so inclined, this preparation could easily take the heat of a few added chiles.

Serves 4

2 cups cooked black beans

2 5-inch-long poblano chiles, roasted, peeled, and seeded

1 small yellow vine-ripened beefsteak tomato

1 small red vine-ripened beefsteak tomato

Salt and pepper

1 small avocado

½ teaspoon lemon juice

1 teaspoon minced shallots

½ cup cooked black-eyed peas

4 teaspoons olive oil

2 small tomatillos

4 slices each oven-dried yellow and red beefsteak tomatoes (recipe follows)

Chervil for garnish

Coriander Juice (recipe follows)

2 tablespoons yellow tomato concassée

2 tablespoons diced oven-dried red tomatoes

METHOD Purée 1½ cups of black beans. Season with salt and pepper. Fill the poblanos with the puréed beans. If the poblanos split open as you peel and seed them, lay them flat on plastic wrap. Lay the purée down on the chiles, roll them back up into their original shape, and wrap in plastic. Refrigerate several hours to set the bean purée, then cut the poblanos in ¼-inch slices. Cut the red and yellow tomatoes into ⅛-inch slices and season with salt and pepper. Peel and dice the avocado, and toss with the lemon juice and shallots. Toss the remaining black beans with the black-eyed peas and 2 teaspoons of olive oil and season to taste. Finely dice the tomatillos and sauté them in 2 teaspoons of olive oil until just soft. Season to taste with salt and pepper.

ASSEMBLY Build a pyramid of tomatoes and stuffed poblanos in each bowl, along with the sautéed tomatillo, avocado, and some of the black bean and black-eyed pea mixture. Top with slices of oven-dried tomatoes. Place some of the bean and pea mixture around the pyramid, and pour about 3 tablespoons of Coriander Juice into each bowl. Garnish with yellow tomato *concassée*, diced oven-dried tomatoes, and chervil.

Oven-Dried Tomatoes

1 large beefsteak tomato
Salt and pepper

METHOD Cut the tomato into ½-inch slices. Season with salt and pepper and lay the slices on a rack over a sheet pan. Bake at 300 degrees for 30 minutes. Gently turn the tomatoes over and continue to bake for another 20 minutes or until the tomatoes are completely dry. Remove from oven and cool.

Coriander Juice

1 bunch coriander, blanched and shocked
2 tablespoons rice vinegar
2 tablespoons grapeseed oil
1 cup cold water
Salt and pepper

METHOD Purée the coriander, rice vinegar, grapeseed oil, and water in a blender. Strain through a fine strainer and season to taste.

Wine Notes

This preparation is hot and spicy, though tempered somewhat by the creaminess of the beans and the avocado. The completing element of the wine should be fruit, and there is no better pure expression of fruit than a young Beaujolais. Georges DuBoeuf's numerous Crus include the light Chiroubles and the elegant Fleurie, and both work well. For a slight Italianate twist, try a Conterno Dolcetto or Freisa, and for light California pleasure, a cool J. Lohr or Robert Pecota Gamay are eminently drinkable fruity red wines.

Clear Gazpacho with Avocado, Jicama, and Apple

This cool, refreshing dish could best be described as part salad, part soup. It has all the components of a typical gazpacho, and then some. The bits of fruit add an interesting sweet element that offsets the heat of the chiles. The delicate yet full-flavored Tomato Water ties everything together so that each element retains its distinct texture and flavor, yet with each spoonful, they combine in your mouth to produce gazpacho.

Serves 4

1 ½ tablespoons finely julienned jicama

1 ½ tablespoons finely julienned zucchini

1 ½ tablespoons finely julienned yellow squash

1 ½ tablespoons finely julienned tomato

1 ½ tablespoons finely julienned red bell pepper

1 tablespoon lemon juice

3 ½ teaspoons olive oil

Salt and pepper

1 tablespoon chopped fennel fronds

1 tablespoon chopped chervil

1 tablespoon chopped opal basil

½ tablespoon chopped coriander

½ tablespoon chopped savory

1 avocado, peeled, pitted, and scooped into Parisienne balls

24 red currant tomatoes

12 yellow currant tomatoes, halved

2 tablespoons peeled and finely diced yellow plums

2 tablespoons finely diced zucchini, blanched

2 tablespoons peeled and finely diced apple

2 tablespoons peeled and finely diced cucumber

2 tablespoons tomato concassée

2 or 3 red jalapeños, finely sliced

Snipped chives

1 ⅓ cups Tomato Water (see Appendix)

METHOD Toss together the julienned jicama, zucchini, yellow squash, tomato, red bell pepper, lemon juice, and 3 teaspoons of olive oil. Season lightly with salt and pepper and chill thoroughly.

Toss together the fennel, chervil, basil, coriander, savory, and ½ teaspoon of olive oil, and season with a few grains of salt.

ASSEMBLY Pack a 1¼-to-1½-inch round cutter with the julienned vegetables in the center of each bowl. Remove the cutter and top each round with a small mound of mixed herbs. Strew the avocado, currant tomatoes, plums, zucchini, apple, cucumber, tomato concassée, and chiles into each bowl. Sprinkle with a few snipped chives. Add ⅓ cup of Tomato Water to each bowl.

Wine Notes

This beautiful, delicate liquid combines mildly sweet flavors of apple and red bell pepper in tiny bursts with the fresh, crunchy vegetable elements. A very light, low-alcohol Mosel Kabinett from a classic vineyard site such as Wehlener Sonnenuhr can make these flavors harmonize beautifully. The delicate sweetness of the wine is balanced by firm acidity, matching the effect of the gazpacho.

Tomato Risotto with Petite Herb Salad and Brown Butter Vinaigrette

In August and September, I usually offer an all-tomato menu that is always received with great enthusiasm. This tomato-flavored risotto works well as an entrée on that menu because it is earthy and substantial. The herb salad and spinach offer a refreshing contrast to the pungent rice. Finally, the Brown Butter Vinaigrette ties all the flavors together with a subtle richness and just the perfect refined acidic edge.

Serves 4

3 tablespoons minced onion

2 teaspoons minced garlic

2 tablespoons unsalted butter

⅔ cup Arborio rice

2 cups Tomato Water (see Appendix)

2 tablespoons tomato paste

2 tablespoons chopped oil-packed sun-dried tomatoes

2 tablespoons tomato concassée

3 tablespoons chopped sautéed spinach

Salt and pepper

½ cup assorted herbs and edible flower petals (chervil, tarragon, chives, lamb's-quarter, violas, pansies, nasturtiums, chive blossoms, etc.)

1 tablespoon olive oil

Brown Butter Vinaigrette (recipe follows)

METHOD In a large pan, sweat the onion and garlic in butter over medium heat until softened and just translucent, about 3 or 4 minutes. Add the Arborio rice and cook, stirring constantly, for 4 to 5 minutes. Add the Tomato Water, ¼ cup at a time, and continue cooking and stirring, allowing the rice to completely absorb the liquid each time before adding more. After you have added 1 cup of liquid (10 minutes or so), stir in the tomato paste, and then continue adding Tomato Water as before, until the rice is just cooked. (It should be al dente yet creamy.) Fold in the sun-dried tomatoes, tomato *concassée*, and sautéed spinach, and season with salt and pepper. Toss the herbs and edible flowers in the olive oil and season to taste with salt and pepper.

ASSEMBLY Spoon a mound of risotto onto the center of each plate or, for a cleaner shape, form in a cutter. Top the risotto with a mound of the herb mixture, and drizzle about 2 tablespoons of Brown Butter Vinaigrette onto each plate.

Brown Butter Vinaigrette

¾ cup unsalted butter

1 tablespoon olive oil

1 tablespoon unsalted butter, softened

4 tablespoons aged balsamic vinegar

Salt and pepper

1 shallot, chopped

METHOD Melt ¾ cup of butter over medium heat in a heavy-bottomed saucepan. Cook over medium heat until the solids separate and fall to the bottom and the butter is a nutty brown color, about 4 to 5 minutes. Remove from heat and let it rest 2 minutes. Skim off any solids remaining on the surface. Pour off the clarified butter and discard the solids on the bottom of the pan. Heat up the clarified butter until it is quite hot and pour it into a blender. With the blender running at medium speed, slowly add the olive oil and softened butter, and blend until well homogenized. With the blender still running, slowly pour in the balsamic vinegar. Season to taste with salt and pepper, whisk in the chopped shallot, and serve immediately. This method will produce an emulsified dressing; if you prefer to allow the oil and vinegar to separate (as in the photograph), whisk the ingredients together gently by hand and allow dressing to sit 2 to 3 minutes before spooning it onto the plate. This recipe makes 1 cup. Extra dressing can be refrigerated. To use again, warm the dressing and reblend if desired.

Wine Notes

This full-flavored earthy dish, with its crunchy texture, slight sweetness, and herbal influences, is best matched with a full-bodied white Burgundy. Many fine examples of Chassagne-Montrachet come from the inimitable Domaine Ramonet, with the somewhat mineral Caillerets Premier Cru nosing out the fruitier Morgeots and firmer Vergers to best complete this preparation.

Terrine of Sliced Heirloom Tomatoes and Eggplant with Tomato Fondant, Chèvre Cream, and Tomato Oil

This tomato terrine makes a wonderful first course. The fascinating thing about it is that the tomato element is present in so many guises—besides forming the base for the terrine, it appears in an intense but ethereal fondant, as a refreshing salad, in the aspic, and in an oil that is redolent of the fruit. The goat cheese cream adds the perfect pungency to what is essentially a very delicate arrangement of flavors. The terrine lends itself to creative interpretation, as one can easily introduce layers of eggplant, artichokes, or other vegetables between the layers of tomato. I use a 10 x 1¼ x 2⅓-inch terrine mold, but other sizes will work as well. Adjust all quantities accordingly, and cut the pieces to fit snugly in the terrine.

Serves 6

5 to 6 large red heirloom tomatoes
5 to 6 large yellow heirloom tomatoes
1 cup Tomato Water (see Appendix)
3 gelatin leaves or 3 teaspoons gelatin granules
Salt and pepper
1 small eggplant
Olive oil
Chèvre Cream (recipe follows)
Tomato Salad (recipe follows)
Tomato Oil (recipe follows)
Tomato Fondant (recipe follows)

METHOD Peel and quarter the tomatoes, and cut away the seeds and core. Cut perfect rectangles 1¾ inches long and as wide as the quartered tomato allows. This is the hardest part of the preparation, but the final result will be worth all the trouble.

To make the tomato aspic, dissolve the gelatin in the Tomato Water and season to taste with salt and pepper. Reserve 2 tablespoons of the aspic for the fondant. It should be at room temperature when construction is ready to begin. Line the terrine mold with plastic wrap. Dip a slice of red tomato into the tomato aspic, shake off excess aspic, and lay the tomato in the mold. Repeat until one layer is complete. Follow this procedure with the yellow tomatoes to create a second layer. Repeat the process, alternating red and yellow layers, until the mold is

almost full. Cover with plastic wrap and refrigerate for at least 2 hours.

Cut about 20 paper-thin lengthwise slices of eggplant. Brush lightly with olive oil, lay them on a nonstick baking sheet, and bake at 350 degrees for 10 minutes. Lay the slices out on plastic wrap, trimming the edges to form an 8 x 10-inch rectangle, and liberally brush the eggplant with tomato aspic. Carefully turn the tomato terrine out onto the eggplant along one 10-inch edge. Carefully roll it up in the eggplant, using the plastic wrap to help mold it around the terrine. Return it to the mold and refrigerate for another hour.

ASSEMBLY Unmold the terrine and cut six ½-inch slices. Spoon a little Chèvre Cream onto the center of each plate. Place a slice of terrine in the center of the cream. Spoon 2 or 3 mounds each of Tomato Fondant and Tomato Salad around the slice of terrine. Drizzle about 1 tablespoon of Tomato Oil around the edges of each plate.

Chèvre Cream

2 ounces chèvre
⅓ cup water

METHOD Purée until completely smooth. Pass through a fine strainer.

Tomato Salad

¼ cup yellow heirloom tomato concassée
¼ cup red heirloom tomato concassée

2 teaspoons chopped basil
1 tablespoon olive oil
1 teaspoon minced garlic
Salt

METHOD Toss all ingredients together and season to taste with salt.

Tomato Oil

2 cups heirloom tomato concassée
2 cups olive oil

METHOD Poach the tomato *concassée* in the olive oil in a 180-degree oven overnight. Strain and discard the tomatoes. Let stand for 1 hour to allow the sediment to fall to the bottom. Decant the oil from the sediment.

Tomato Fondant

1 medium onion, diced
2 cloves garlic, chopped
2 teaspoons grapeseed oil
4 large beefsteak tomatoes, chopped
Salt and pepper
2 tablespoons tomato paste
1 tablespoon sugar
Pinch of saffron
6 large basil leaves
1 cup heavy cream, whipped to full peaks
2 tablespoons tomato aspic at room temperature (from above terrine recipe)

METHOD In a medium sauté pan, sauté the onion and garlic in the grapeseed oil until

soft. Add the tomatoes and salt and pepper to taste and slowly cook over low heat, stirring frequently, until most of the liquid is evaporated. Press through a fine mesh strainer into a heavy-bottomed saucepan. Add the tomato paste, sugar, saffron, and basil. Cover and cook over low heat, stirring occasionally until it reaches the consistency of tomato paste. Remove basil leaves, adjust seasoning, and allow to cool. Fold the tomato aspic into the whipped cream. Fold approximately ½ to ¾ cup of the tomato reduction into the cream mixture, using more or less depending on the desired density. Keep cool until ready to serve.

Wine Notes

Heirloom tomatoes have a sweetness that is extended by the Chèvre Cream and the fondant, yet the natural acidity of tomatoes needs a firmly acidic wine. As an early course, this terrine will work well with a lighter-bodied, crisp wine. Chablis provides an excellent backbone of acidity to match up to the tomatoes: a dry Premier Cru Vaillons from Moreau or Laroche makes a fine companion, while freshening the palate with each sip.

Roasted Tomatoes Stuffed with Couscous, Chanterelles, and Pine Nuts

This is an especially simple dish to prepare and to serve. I merely take tomatoes that have been hollowed out and roasted, fill them with a tabboulehlike salad, and heat them up in the oven for a few minutes. They work perfectly as a course by themselves or as an accompaniment to salmon or swordfish.

Serves 4

*8 small heirloom tomatoes
(e.g., Yellow Taxi, Cherokee, or Valerie)*

2 to 3 tablespoons Herb Oil (see Appendix)

8 cloves garlic

8 thyme sprigs

8 tarragon sprigs

8 bay leaves

8 large basil leaves

1 cup cooked couscous

2 tablespoons quartered, sautéed chanterelle mushrooms

1 tablespoon tomato concassée

1 tablespoon roasted pine nuts

1 tablespoon finely diced peeled cucumber

1 tablespoon sautéed sweet corn kernels

1 tablespoon olive oil

1 teaspoon chopped chives

1 teaspoon chopped tarragon

1 teaspoon chopped mint

1 teaspoon opal basil, cut into a chiffonade

Salt and pepper

16 chive pieces, about 2 inches long

METHOD Peel the tomatoes and cut a ¾-inch slice off the bottom of each, reserving them for *lids*. Scoop out the seeds and the center flesh. Rub the insides with a little Herb Oil, and put a clove of garlic, a sprig of thyme, a sprig of tarragon, a bay leaf, and a basil leaf in each tomato. Put the lids on and roast at 325 degrees for 10 to 12 minutes or until the tomatoes just begin to soften (not so long that they lose their shape). Remove and discard the garlic and herbs. Warm the couscous over a double boiler and stir in the mushrooms, tomatoes, pine nuts, cucumber, and corn one at a time until they are all thoroughly incorporated. Stir in the olive oil, chopped chives, tarragon, mint, and basil, and season to taste with salt and pepper. Spoon the warm couscous salad into the hot tomatoes and top with the lids. Rub the tomatoes with a little Herb Oil and return them to the oven for 5 minutes.

ASSEMBLY Place 2 tomatoes on each plate, garnish each with 2 chive pieces, and serve.

Wine Notes

The sweetness attained by the tomatoes when they are roasted makes them an excellent vehicle for the additional rich flavors of pine nuts and chanterelles. This complex tomato dish, made more substantial by the couscous, will stand up to a medium-bodied red wine. The mint and basil suggest an herbally influenced wine, like Estancia's Sangiovese from the Alexander Valley. The fruitiness of this wine works well, while its zesty finish resolves the sweet tomato flavors.

POTATOES

During the month of January, and on into February, I often feature on our vegetable menu an all-potato dinner profiling different potatoes prepared in a variety of ways. Most people think of potatoes in terms of russets and white or red new potatoes, not realizing that there are many other kinds now readily available, such as the fingerlings and golden-fleshed varieties (Yukon golds and Finnish yellows, for instance). They each differ slightly in texture, water content, thickness of skin, creaminess, starchiness, and color. Add to that the fact that the texture of a potato can change dramatically depending upon whether it is fried, roasted, puréed, poached, or creamed, and I would have to say that potatoes are one of our most versatile foodstuffs.

Most often I use potatoes to highlight other foods; I especially like to use them with such luxury items as truffles or caviar. Sometimes, though, potatoes can be a tremendous focal point. In the following recipes you will find them wonderful in a supporting role or as the main item.

Potato and Eggplant Terrine with Goat Cheese Fondant, Beet and Parsley Juices, and Curry Oil

*I first featured this visually stunning dish on an all-potato menu that I served at the
James Beard House in New York in January 1990. The potato and eggplant in the terrine are perfectly
complemented by a delicate Goat Cheese Fondant and a touch of fragrant Curry Oil.
The mushroom salad and the Beet Juice offer earthy elements that add a fantastic complement to
a very light combination of ingredients. Like most terrines, this one can be made ahead,
then sliced and served at the last moment. The terrine can be prepared as described below, or for an even
more arresting presentation, can be wrapped in a layer of blanched spinach leaves (see page 76.).*

Serves 4

3 Idaho potatoes, peeled
1½ tablespoons olive oil
Salt and pepper
1 medium eggplant
½ tablespoon chopped parsley
Goat Cheese Fondant (recipe follows)
¼ cup thinly sliced shiitake mushrooms
1 teaspoon snipped chives
Beet Juice (see Appendix)
Parsley Juice (see Appendix)
Curry Oil (recipe follows)

METHOD Slice the potatoes lengthwise into ⅓-inch-thick slices, then cut the slices into 2-inch widths or to fit the width of your terrine. Rub them with a little olive oil and lightly season with salt and pepper. Place the slices on a parchment-lined sheet pan and bake at 350 degrees for 20 to 25 minutes or until they are just cooked through. Cool at room temperature. Cut the eggplant in half lengthwise, rub the cut sides with a little olive oil, and place on a roasting pan, cut side down. Prick the skin a couple of times with a sharp fork and bake for 20 to 30 minutes at 425 degrees until the eggplant is soft. Scoop out the pulp and pass it through a food mill. Heat the pulp in a double boiler and evaporate away some of the liquid to thicken it and concentrate the flavor. Allow to cool at room temperature, then fold in the parsley and season with salt and pepper.

Very lightly oil a 2 x 9 x 2½-inch terrine mold and line it with plastic wrap. Place a layer of potatoes in the bottom of the mold and spread it with some of the eggplant mixture. Continue to add alternate layers of potato and eggplant until the mold is almost filled. Wrap it tightly with plastic wrap and refrigerate for at least 2 hours. (This much can be done a day in advance.)

For the mushroom salad, sauté the mushrooms in the remaining olive oil over medium-high heat for 3 to 4 minutes or until they are thoroughly cooked. Cool and toss in the chives.

ASSEMBLY Cut 4 slices of the terrine (there will be more than enough terrine for 4 servings, but it is difficult to make anything less). For each serving, place a slice of terrine in the center of the plate. Place 3 quenelles of Goat Cheese Fondant around the slice of terrine, alternating with scoops of mushroom salad. Drizzle a little of the Beet Juice, Parsley Juice, and Curry Oil around the edges of the plate.

Goat Cheese Fondant

4 ounces goat cheese
½ cup heavy cream
Salt and white pepper

METHOD Soften the cheese to room temperature. Place in a pan and beat with a spatula to smooth it, then continue stirring over low, even heat until it is very smooth and the graininess is gone. Whip the cream to soft peaks and fold into the cheese. Season with salt and white pepper and place over ice to set. Using small spoons, shape into 12 quenelles.

Curry Oil

½ cup chopped onion
½ cup chopped apple
2 cups plus 2 tablespoons grapeseed oil
¼ cup curry powder
2 teaspoons turmeric
Salt and pepper

METHOD Over medium heat, sauté the onion and apple in 2 tablespoons of grapeseed oil until just translucent. Season with salt and pepper. Add the curry powder and turmeric and cook until the mixture starts to get pasty. Add the remaining grapeseed oil, mix well, and continue to cook until the oil is warm (do not boil). Thoroughly purée in a blender, pour into a container, and cover. Refrigerate for 2 days. Decant carefully.

Wine Notes

Young Châteauneuf-du-Pape Blanc, brimming with ripe, warm-climate fruit, will complement the complex array of vegetable flavors found here. Curry provides just the right lift of flavor for the richness of this style of wine, and the earthy, hearty eggplant works naturally with this wine from the southern Rhône Valley. The finest examples are from Domaine Vieux Télégraphe and Château de Beaucastel, especially its rare Roussanne *Vieilles Vignes*. For a fruitier accompaniment, a dry Riesling from Alsace will push flavor forward while not dominating the dish. Try a mature Trimbach *Cuvée Frédéric Emile*.

Belgian Endive, Frisée, Watercress, Crispy Potatoes, and Potato Cream

At the restaurant I always offer some type of salad with bitter, sharp, buttery, and
spicy greens. Various versions have appeared—in combination with fruits, nuts, or goat cheese,
for instance—but this one may be my favorite rendition. The crispy potatoes and rich,
satiny Potato Cream act as the perfect backdrop for the greens and the endive.
This could be served either after the main course or somewhere in the middle of the meal.
Black truffle may be added for a luxurious touch!

Serves 4

2 small heads Belgian endive

4 chives, blanched

1 to 2 potatoes cut into 32 bâtonets

2 tablespoons hazelnut oil

½ cup frisée

½ cup watercress

½ cup red oak leaf lettuce, mâche,
or Boston lettuce, torn in small pieces

Potato Cream (recipe follows)

2 tablespoons halved or slivered
almonds, roasted

1 tablespoon julienned black truffle
(optional)

Salt and pepper

METHOD Julienne the Belgian endive lengthwise and divide it into 4 piles. Using the blanched chives, tie each mound of endive about one-third of the way up into a little bundle. In a nonstick pan over medium-high heat, sauté the potatoes in 2 teaspoons of hazelnut oil until golden and crispy. Remove to paper towels and blot off excess oil.

ASSEMBLY Spread 2 tablespoons of Potato Cream on the center of each plate. Set an endive bundle upright in the pool of cream, and spread the strands a bit. Arrange the crispy potatoes and the greens around the Belgian endive. Strew the almonds (and optional truffles) around the greens. Drizzle a few drops of hazelnut oil onto the greens and lightly season each salad with salt and pepper.

Potato Cream

1 Idaho russet potato, peeled and grated

1½ cups heavy cream

METHOD Steep the potatoes in the cream over low heat for 30 minutes. Strain and season with salt and pepper. The cream will thicken as it cools because of the starch from the potato, so a touch of water may be necessary to achieve a proper consistency. This can be made up to a day ahead and refrigerated, but should be brought back to room temperature before serving.

Wine Notes

The inclusion of potatoes and almonds in this salad makes the dish richer and more substantial than the typical green salad, though the bitter greens still provide a formidable obstacle to any wine. Sauvignon Blanc seems a natural here, though Sancerre is too lean and many American versions are too herbal. Oak aging can mellow Sauvignon elegantly, while preserving its freshness. Tom Rochioli, in Sonoma's Russian River Valley, grows beautifully textured Sauvignon and handles it gently, producing a fine, dry, almost honeyed wine that could work well here. This wine is especially successful if the salad is served early or mid-meal. If it is served after the main course, the most refreshing way to enjoy it is with still mineral water.

Potato, Butternut Squash, and Black Truffle "Risotto" with Foie Gras and Chicken Stock Reduction

*This dish was inspired by a very similar one that Jeremiah Tower and Mark Franz
prepared at the Chappellet Winery's 25th anniversary celebration in Napa Valley, California.
The whole meal was glorious, but their potato risotto, a brunoise of potatoes prepared
to perfectly emulate Arborio rice, was one of the highlights. The potatoes were thoroughly cooked,
but creamy and ever so slightly al dente. Jeremiah served it with lamb shanks, but here
I have substituted foie gras. Either way, the results are incredible.*

Serves 4

*2 large Idaho potatoes, peeled and cut into a
brunoise*

2 cups Blond Vegetable Stock (see Appendix)

*½ cup roasted butternut squash, cut into a
brunoise*

1 ounce black truffle, cut into a brunoise

1 tablespoon snipped parsley

Salt and pepper

4 1½-ounce pieces of foie gras

*⅓ cup Chicken Stock Reduction
(see Appendix)*

METHOD Place the potato and ⅔ cup
Blond Vegetable Stock in a large sauté pan,
turn the heat to medium, and slowly steam
off the stock, stirring slowly and carefully
to keep the potatoes from disintegrating.
Add another ⅔ cup of the stock and repeat.
Add the remaining stock, butternut squash,
and black truffle. Continue cooking, stirring slowly and carefully, until the remaining stock is gone, about 30 to 40 minutes
total cooking time. Stir in parsley and carefully season to taste. Season the foie gras
pieces lightly on both sides with salt and
pepper. In a small sauté pan over medium-
high heat, sear the foie gras pieces on both
sides until browned. Warm the Chicken
Stock Reduction.

ASSEMBLY Divide the *risotto* onto 4 warm
plates. Place the pieces of foie gras on the
risotto and drizzle a little of the Chicken
Stock Reduction around the edges.

Wine Notes

Red Burgundy seems appropriate here,
highlighting the truffles' aromatic excite-
ment and the sweetness of the squash. Be
sure to choose a wine that is mature, and
from a sound vintage. Numerous great
Burgundies were produced in 1985, among
them the exotically perfumed and sensu-
ously sweet Morey St.-Denis by Georges
Lignier. This wine is at perfect maturity
now, and should be sound for several years.
Another excellent choice is the velvety 1986
Chambolle-Musigny *Les Amoureuses* by
Robert Groffier.

Langoustine Brandade Galette with Crispy Shallots and Basil-Infused Sweet Corn Broth

I have always loved brandade of salt cod in any form. One easy way to make it more elegant is to fold in a little shellfish meat at the last moment—langoustine, scallops, shrimp, or lobster, for instance. In this creation I use langoustine, and the brandade is formed into small galettes which are sautéed to achieve a contrasting crispness. The mousselike codfish mixture is hearty yet delicate enough to perfectly showcase the langoustine, corn, and basil elements.

Serves 4

⅔ cup salt cod

⅔ cup peeled, boiled potato

4 cloves Roasted Garlic (see Appendix)

2½ tablespoons olive oil

2½ tablespoons heavy cream

1 tablespoon chopped parsley

⅔ cup raw, coarsely chopped langoustine meat

Salt and pepper

5½ tablespoons unsalted butter

1½ cups thinly sliced shallots

1 cup Sweet Corn Broth (see Appendix)

½ tablespoon flour

3 cups grapeseed oil

½ cup coarsely chopped basil

6 ears baby corn

Tiny green and purple basil leaves for garnish

METHOD Soak the salt cod in repeated changes of cold water over a 48-hour period. Starting with enough cold, unsalted water to cover, bring the water to a boil and strain immediately. Repeat this process 3 or 4 times or until the salty flavor is gone and the fish is tender. Do not let the fish boil or it will become tough. While it is still warm, place the codfish in an electric mixer with a paddle attachment and slowly beat it at medium speed to fluff. After about a minute add the warm potato, bit by bit, until it is fully incorporated. Beat in the garlic, then with the mixer still at medium speed, slowly drizzle in the olive oil, then the cream. Fold in the parsley and the langoustine meat, and season to taste with salt and pepper. Form 4 equal-sized galettes (for a precise shape, form and sauté them in a 3-inch ring or cutter). In a large nonstick pan, sauté them over medium heat on both sides in 2 tablespoons of butter until they are browned and heated all the way through, about 4 or 5 minutes on each side.

In a small saucepan over medium heat, slowly stew 1 cup of shallots in 2 tablespoons of butter and 2 tablespoons of Sweet Corn Broth until thoroughly softened, about 8 to 10 minutes. Season with salt and pepper. While the shallots are stewing, toss the remaining shallots in the ½ tablespoon of flour and then fry them in the grapeseed oil. Drain them on paper towels and season to taste with salt and pepper.

Bring the remaining Sweet Corn Broth to a boil and steep the basil in it for 20 seconds. Strain immediately and discard the basil. Just before serving, bring the corn broth back to a boil, whisk in the remaining 1½ tablespoons of butter, and adjust the seasonings. Blanch the baby corn in boiling, salted water for 30 seconds, and slice each one into quarters lengthwise.

ASSEMBLY Put some stewed shallots in each bowl, and place a brandade galette on top of the shallots. Strew baby corn pieces around the edges of the bowl and place some fried shallots on top of each galette. Strew a few basil leaves on and around the galettes and pour about ¼ cup of hot basil-infused Sweet Corn Broth into each bowl.

Wine Notes

This dish presents a number of sweet elements, including shallots, sweet corn, and the crustacean itself, that warrant the selection of a fairly intense, ripe, full-bodied white wine. American Chardonnay provides a wide field to choose from, but the best come from several Santa Barbara County producers, like Babcock and Au Bon Climat. Their wines convey a great balance of fruit and oak, but are not ponderous. Other producers of note in the area are Byron, Sanford, Qupé, and Talley, in the Arroyo Grande Valley.

Potato and Truffle Torte with Veal Stock Reduction

*This recipe is based on a dish I had for lunch one day at the Veuve Clicquot
residence in Reims, France. My dear friend Mireille Guiliano of Clicquot had arranged for
Chef Michel Trama to come and prepare a truffle luncheon for our group. Trama wrapped
small potatoes in cabbage rather than pastry, as I do, but the effect is much the same: unmitigated
extravagance of the highest order in a stunning presentation. This could easily work
as a main course, or, as Trama served it, as a little starch course before the finale. Either way
this dish is a winner. Another plus: you can do all the work in advance.*

Serves 4

*4 2-inch-long oval Petit Rosette potatoes,
unpeeled*

1 cup Sweet Corn Broth (see Appendix)

2 tablespoons unsalted butter

2 to 3 ounces black truffles, thinly sliced

*4 tablespoons Herb Compound Butter,
softened (recipe follows)*

*20 large spinach leaves, cleaned
and stemmed*

Brioche (recipe follows)

Egg wash

*½ to ¾ cup Veal Stock Reduction
(see Appendix)*

*Chopped herbs (e.g., basil, tarragon,
rosemary, thyme, etc.)*

METHOD Boil the potatoes in lightly salted water for 6 to 7 minutes until they just begin to soften. Remove them from the water and allow to cool to room temperature. While the potatoes are cooling, heat the Sweet Corn Broth, stir in the butter, and when it has melted, lightly poach the truffle slices for a minute or so in the hot broth. Remove the truffle slices and reduce the broth to about 3 tablespoons. Set it aside and reserve for the sauce.

Carefully blanch the spinach leaves in boiling water for about 15 seconds. Drain and pat dry. Lay out 4 sheets of plastic wrap, each 12 inches square. On each, arrange 5 spinach leaves to create a circle 8 to 10 inches in diameter. Cut each unpeeled potato into 6 slices, arranging the slices side by side in order. Lay a few truffle slices on top of each slice except the last one, and spread each with about ½ teaspoon softened Herb Compound Butter. (Use about ¼

of the truffles on each potato.) Re-form the potatoes by stacking the slices back up in order. Carefully wrap each potato in spinach, using the plastic wrap to help mold the spinach tightly around the potato. Refrigerate for 45 minutes to 1 hour to firm.

Using Brioche dough, roll out 4 circles 8 to 10 inches in diameter. Remove the plastic wrap from the potatoes and then wrap each potato in dough, pinching off any excess dough. Refrigerate the Brioche-wrapped potatoes for at least 1 hour or until ready to bake. Brush with an egg wash after ½ hour and again when you are ready to cook them. Bake at 450 degrees for 7 to 8 minutes or until golden brown and hot in the center. Warm the Veal Stock Reduction and whisk in the reduced Sweet Corn Broth.

ASSEMBLY Spoon 2 to 3 tablespoons of the Veal Stock Reduction onto each plate. Slice the tortes in half lengthwise and place 2 halves in the center of each plate. Sprinkle chopped herbs around the plate.

Brioche

1 tablespoon yeast

¼ cup sugar

4 tablespoons warm water

6 eggs

1 tablespoon kosher salt

4 cups flour

2 cups butter, softened

METHOD Dissolve the yeast and half the sugar in the warm water. Beat the eggs with the remaining sugar and the salt. Sift the flour onto a table and make a well. Pour the yeast and eggs into the well. Mix with

fingertips until well combined. The dough will be moist and sticky. Knead for several minutes. Cut in the butter. Place the dough in an oiled bowl and cover with plastic wrap. Punch down after dough has doubled in size (about 1 to 2 hours). The dough is now ready to use.

Herb Compound Butter

1 cup unsalted butter, softened

¼ cup finely chopped parsley

1 tablespoon finely chopped chives

1 teaspoon finely chopped tarragon

1 teaspoon finely chopped sage

1 teaspoon finely chopped rosemary

1 teaspoon finely chopped chervil

1 teaspoon lemon juice

Salt and pepper

METHOD Combine the ingredients in a mixer or food processor and refrigerate.

Wine Notes

This intensely perfumed dish is visually and aromatically stunning. A mature wine of Rioja or the Ribera del Duero region in Spain will project wonderful vanilla aromas alongside cedar and cherry characteristics to enrich the dish. Tempranillo, the principal grape variety of these regions, requires time to soften but is often reminiscent of Pinot Noir's delicacy and refinement. The only caution in the flavor matching here would be the spinach in the preparation, which could be too bitter if only lightly blanched. A great example of mature Rioja is the La Rioja Alta Centenario 1973; the great Vega Sicilia Unico 1980 would be a stunning complement as well, though an even rarer treat would be the 1968.

Roasted Fingerling Potatoes with Osetra Caviar and Crème Fraîche

Fingerling potatoes are quite buttery, almost creamy, in fact, and because of this, they work incredibly well when paired with caviar. I like this particular dish because it teams up two opposites—the humble potato with luxurious caviar—and does it in a way that enhances the virtues of both. Beyond the almost perfect match of flavors in this rather unusual combination, there is the startling temperature contrast—piping hot potatoes played off against the cold caviar and crème fraîche.

Serves 4

2 hard-boiled eggs

20 to 24 small fingerling potatoes, scrubbed but not peeled

6 tablespoons unsalted butter

4 or 5 medium shallots, peeled and coarsely chopped

¼ cup chopped parsley

Herb Oil (see Appendix)

Salt and pepper

6 tablespoons crème fraîche

4 ounces Osetra caviar

METHOD Separate the egg whites from the yolks. Chop the whites, and pass the yolks through a sieve; set aside. In an ovenproof sauté pan over medium heat, sauté the potatoes in 4 tablespoons of butter for 2 or 3 minutes. Place the pan in a 450-degree oven for 7 to 9 minutes, flipping the potatoes over after 3 minutes or so. When the potatoes are thoroughly cooked, season them with salt and pepper and remove them to a paper towel to blot off excess oil. While the potatoes are baking, sauté the shallots in the remaining butter over medium heat for 6 to 8 minutes or until they just begin to caramelize. Remove them to a paper towel to blot off excess fat. Season with salt and pepper.

ASSEMBLY Place a small mound of shallots in the center of each plate. Form a circle of egg whites around the shallots. Spoon the yolks around the whites, then sprinkle parsley around the yolks. Drizzle a tablespoon or so of Herb Oil around the edges of each plate. Place 4 or 5 potatoes on top of the shallots. Top with 1½ tablespoons of crème fraîche and 1 ounce of caviar.

Wine Notes

One cannot argue with the choice of a classic match: great Champagne. Krug Vintage 1982 presents fabulous rich flavors that seem custom-made for the luxury of caviar, while also integrating the earthy component of the fingerling potatoes. Other *tête de cuvée* Champagnes will also perform admirably, such as Bollinger R.D. and Salon *Le Mesnil* 1982. These are particularly attractive as the starting point of a great meal.

MUSHROOMS

Mushrooms are the quintessential foodstuff of the earth, and as close to meat in terms of texture and flavor as to any of the other vegetables I work with. Each type has its own unique qualities: some are quite pungent while others have a soft perfume; some have a chewier texture, while others are softer and just melt in your mouth. Some, like the morel and the portobella, are better in starring roles, while the milder ones—the shiitakes and matsutakes, or even the common button mushroom—are excellent in minor roles. Mushrooms can taste of straw, wheat, even nuts, and they respond well to almost any cooking technique.

Throughout the year, as different varieties go in and out of season, the possibilities are endless. In the following recipes, depending upon their season and availability, most wild mushrooms may be substituted for one another, resulting in interesting variations on the themes I have composed. I use the term *wild* a bit loosely here, since many of the so-called wild mushrooms available at the typical market are really cultivated exotic mushrooms. They can be quite nice, and certainly make suitable substitutes. Nevertheless, your palate will be well served if you make the effort to secure truly wild, just-foraged mushrooms.

Truffled Exotic Mushroom and Root Vegetable Tart with Red Wine Butter Sauce

This recipe is one of the rare instances in which I use a classically prepared butter sauce.
Normally I do not like the richness of so much butter, but in this case it is hard to top the combination
of the intensely flavored Red Wine Butter Sauce and the wonderful roasted mushrooms
encased in the flaky pastry. Among the joys of living in the Midwest are the frequent
cold winter nights when a dish such as this would hit the spot.

Eight 5-inch tarts

½ pound shiitake mushrooms, cleaned and stemmed

½ pound tree oyster mushrooms, cleaned

½ pound crimini mushrooms, cleaned and stemmed

½ pound portobella mushrooms, cleaned and stemmed

1 head garlic, cut in half

1 bunch fresh thyme

1½ cups Chicken or Vegetable Stock (see Appendix)

6 baby carrots, peeled and halved

6 baby corn, cleaned and halved

6 baby turnips, peeled and halved

6 baby squash, halved

¼ cup white truffle oil

½ fennel bulb, cut into bâtonnets

1 salsify root, peeled and cut on a bias into ¼-inch slices

Salt and white pepper

2 tablespoons julienned black truffles (optional, for an extra-special occasion)

6 cups unbleached flour

2¼ cups unsalted butter

1 tablespoon kosher salt

About 1 cup ice water

Egg wash (optional)

Red Wine Butter Sauce (recipe follows)

METHOD Cut any very large mushrooms into pieces of about 1 to 1½ inches. Place the mushrooms in a small roasting pan with the garlic, thyme, and stock. Cover with foil and roast at 400 degrees for 10 minutes. Remove from the oven and strain, reserving the liquid, cover and continue to roast for an additional 10 minutes. Gently squeeze the mushrooms and garlic, adding the resulting juice to the reserved liquid. Cool the mushrooms and discard the garlic.

Blanch the carrots, corn, turnips, squash, fennel, and salsify in salt water until half cooked. Shock them in an ice bath, drain thoroughly, and toss with the truffle oil. Reduce the reserved mushroom juice to about 3 concentrated tablespoons and toss with the mushrooms and the vegetable mixture. Lightly season to taste with salt and pepper. (Note: Hot food needs less seasoning than cold, so be careful not to overseason.)

For the dough, cut butter roughly into ½-inch dice and refrigerate. Sift the flour and salt into a large mixing bowl. With your hands, quickly work the butter into the flour until the mixture forms small balls. Using only as much as needed to make the dough come together, work cold water into the dough. Be sure not to overmix; the dough should still have visible pieces of butter. Let the dough rest for ½ hour.

Butter and flour 8 4- to 5-inch tart pans with removable bottoms. Roll half the dough out to a thickness of ¹/₁₆ inch. Cut 8 circles 7 inches in diameter, and line the pans with dough. Adjust the seasoning in the filling if necessary. Spoon in the filling, packing the pans full. Roll out remaining dough, cut out 8 slightly smaller circles, and cover the mushrooms with pastry. Seal the edges closed. Refrigerate for an hour or two. At this point, brushing the pastry with a simple egg wash will create a glazed effect when the pastry is baked, but it is entirely optional. Cut a small vent into the top of each tartlet. Bake at 400 degrees for 20 to 30 minutes or until golden.

ASSEMBLY Spoon some of the Red Wine Butter Sauce onto each plate, unmold the tarts onto the plates, and serve.

Red Wine Butter Sauce

2 shallots, peeled and chopped

½ cup plus 2 tablespoons butter

1 small tomato, concassée

4 tablespoons aged balsamic vinegar

3 cups red wine (preferably Cabernet)

1 tablespoon heavy cream

Salt and pepper

METHOD Sweat the shallots in 2 tablespoons of butter until thoroughly softened. Add the tomato and balsamic vinegar and reduce to a glaze. Add the red wine and reduce to 1 cup. Strain and reduce to ¼ cup. Add the cream and then whisk in the remaining butter bit by bit. Season with salt and pepper.

Wine Notes

The red wine sauce and the heartiness of the vegetable and mushroom elements of this satisfying preparation point only to a classical style of red wine. Burgundy always seems to make sense in conjunction with wild mushrooms, and, indeed, a firm but somewhat mature wine like the Morey St.-Denis from Roumier in 1988 is a fine match. Equally interesting would be the way a traditional Sangiovese from Tuscany, like the Il Sodaccio of Monte Vertine, or the Flaccianello by the great Chianti house of Fontodi, would drape the tart in earthy, dried-fruit elegance.

Wild Mushroom Ragoût
with Chicken Stock Reduction

*Although this dish is quite simple to prepare, it is anything but simple on the palate, as each
variety of mushroom used adds its unique qualities to the whole, resulting in an earthy,
soul-satisfying preparation of sublime complexity. It makes a wonderful main course and needs
virtually no accompaniment other than perhaps a salad and a side of quinoa.*

Serves 4

*½ pound shiitake mushrooms, cleaned and
stemmed*

*½ pound cinnamon cap mushrooms, cleaned
and stemmed*

*½ pound white trumpet mushrooms, cleaned
and stemmed*

*½ pound hedgehog mushrooms, cleaned and
stemmed*

*½ pound cèpe mushrooms, cleaned and
stemmed*

½ cup unsalted butter

6 tablespoons Madeira

Salt and pepper

Tarragon leaves

Chopped parsley

*½ cup Chicken Stock Reduction
(see Appendix)*

METHOD Cut any very large mushrooms
into smaller pieces to have some consistency in size. Stirring occasionally, carefully sauté the mushrooms in butter over
medium heat for 10 minutes or until they
are just cooked and the liquid has evaporated. Deglaze with the Madeira and cook
until it evaporates. Season with salt and
pepper and toss in the tarragon leaves and
parsley. Warm the Chicken Stock Reduction in a small saucepan.

ASSEMBLY Divide the mushrooms onto 4
warm plates and spoon 2 or 3 tablespoons
of the Chicken Stock Reduction on top of
each mound of mushrooms.

Wine Notes

A meaty richness pervades this dish, whose
central cèpe flavors are as hedonistically
pleasing as foie gras. That said, this is a versatile dish for which both red and white
wines work. Red selections would include
many Pinot Noirs from Oregon, more delicate Côte de Beaune reds, and some meaty
Pinots from California's Central Coast.
Calera's Reed and Mills Vineyards present
a fine foil. On the white side, Zind-
Humbrecht's Pinot Gris Vieilles Vignes
1990 can also match up well. A crisper,
more austere Alsace producer, or a Mosel or
Rhine wine, might not carry the richness
needed for these gorgeous mushrooms.

Mushroom Noodles with Vermouth and Braised Lettuce Sauce

This preparation has a definite heartiness because of the pasta and the mushrooms, but at the same time a very delicate quality is present. This is due to the wilted lettuce and the little bit of vermouth that make up the sauce. The dish could work as a first course or could easily be the focal point if a larger portion were served. Vegetable Stock could be substituted for the Chicken Stock, resulting in a vegetarian preparation.

Serves 4

4½ tablespoons unsalted butter

⅔ cup tiny chanterelle mushrooms, cleaned and halved

⅔ cup tiny hon she meji mushrooms, cleaned

2 small shallots, peeled and sliced into rings

5 tablespoons dry vermouth

½ cup Chicken Stock (see Appendix)

Salt and pepper

1 head Boston lettuce, all leaves removed and separated, outer leaves discarded

Chanterelle Noodles (recipe follows)

Shiitake Noodles (recipe follows)

Chopped herbs

Snipped chives

METHOD In a medium sauté pan, melt 1½ tablespoons of butter over medium heat. Stirring frequently, sauté the mushrooms and shallots until they are thoroughly softened and quite browned, about 8 to 10 minutes. Deglaze with the vermouth and reduce by half. Add the Chicken Stock and immediately stir in 1 tablespoon of butter. Season with salt and pepper. Add the lettuce leaves and just barely wilt them in the stock, about 45 to 60 seconds.

In the meantime, cook the pastas in two separate pots of boiling, salted water. Drain and place in separate bowls. Add 1 tablespoon of butter to each bowl, season with salt and pepper, and toss on a few herbs.

ASSEMBLY Place a mound of each type of noodles onto each of 4 warm plates. Top with mushrooms and lettuce, and drizzle on the sauce. Garnish with snipped chives.

Chanterelle Noodles

1 cup chanterelle mushrooms, cleaned
¼ cup water (or more if necessary)
1 egg yolk
¼ to 1½ cups semolina flour

METHOD Thoroughly blend the mushrooms with the water until you have a smooth purée. In a double boiler, evaporate as much liquid as possible out of the mushrooms. This will take up to 1½ hours and you will need to stir and scrape the sides with a rubber spatula frequently (you can do this in a sauté pan, but you must be very careful not to burn it). You should end with about ⅓ to ½ cup concentrated purée. Cool down the purée and beat in the yolk. Work in enough flour to form a loose ball. Allow to rest for at least 1 hour. Roll out by hand or with a pasta machine. Cut into fettucini or other desired shape, and refrigerate on a clean, floured kitchen towel until ready to use.

Shiitake Noodles

Follow the recipe for Chanterelle Noodles, substituting 1 cup of cleaned shiitake mushrooms for the chanterelles.

Wine Notes

Here the woodsy pastas maintain their own identities, and the mushrooms in the Chicken Stock preparation bridge the chanterelle and shiitake flavors. The wilted lettuce adds a textural balance that does not interfere with potential wine flavors. A mature white Rhône wine (of at least 10 years' age), such as a Chavé Hermitage Blanc, will have evolved a fascinating bottle bouquet that would elevate and support the mushroom noodles. This is particularly appropriate if the course is an early one. If it is a main course, perhaps a wine of more intensity could be served, like a mature red Corton from Prince de Mérode. Another wonderful possibility is a Nuits-St.-Georges by Robert Chevillon.

Wild Mushroom and Potato Pavé with Tomato Coulis, Red Wine Reduction, and Herb Oil

This dish has been on and off the menu since the very early days of the restaurant.
It can be made with practically any type of wild or fresh mushrooms, but because of their headiness,
I think the chanterelles work best. This is a tremendous make-ahead dish. The pavé can be
made a day or so beforehand, cut hours before you need it, and sautéed just at the last moment.
In addition, because it literally goes from sauté pan to plate, it works wonderfully
as a transition between more complex courses.

Serves 6

3 large Idaho potatoes, peeled

½ cup heavy cream

½ pound chanterelle mushrooms, cleaned and coarsely chopped

1 tablespoon unsalted butter

1½ tablespoons chopped parsley

Salt and pepper

Oil and additional butter for pan

Grapeseed oil

Tomato Coulis (see Appendix)

Red Wine Reduction (see Appendix)

Herb Oil (see Appendix)

METHOD Using a mandolin or a Chinese cleaver, slice the potatoes as thinly as possible lengthwise and soak them in the cream to coat them and prevent oxidation. Sauté the mushrooms in the butter over medium heat for about 10 minutes, stirring frequently. Transfer to a food processor and pulse several times until the mushrooms are thoroughly puréed. Return them to the sauté pan and continue to cook over medium heat for another 5 minutes or so, to evaporate most of the excess moisture. Remove from the heat, stir in the parsley, and season with salt and pepper.

Lightly oil a 3 x 6 x 2-inch baking pan, line it carefully with foil, and thoroughly butter the foil. Remove the potato slices one by one from the cream, shaking off the excess and leaving just the barest coating. Arrange a double layer of potatoes on the bottom of the pan. Spoon on ⅓ of the mushrooms and spread them into a thin layer. Repeat 2 more times, then end with a double layer of potatoes (there should be 4 layers of potato and 3 layers of mushrooms in all). Cut a piece of foil slightly larger than the pan, butter the shiny side, and lay it on top of the potatoes to completely cover. Lay a second baking pan on top of the foil and weight it with a brick or some other heavy, ovenproof object. Bake at 375 degrees for 1 hour. Leaving the weight on top, cool at room temperature at least 2 hours, then refrigerate for at least 6 to 8 hours, preferably overnight. Before serving, remove the foil and cut into 1½ x 2-inch squares or into any desired shape. Over medium heat, sauté the squares in a little grapeseed oil for 3 to 4 minutes. Turn them over and brown them on the other side. Return them to the baking pan and place in a 375-degree oven for 10 to 12 minutes or until warmed through.

ASSEMBLY Drizzle the Tomato Coulis, Red Wine Reduction, and Herb Oil onto the plates (squeeze bottles work well for this). Blot the excess oil off the pavés, and place them on the plates.

Wine Notes

The chanterelles in this preparation constitute a delicate element, with the potatoes providing structure and the Tomato Coulis adding a slight sweetness to the whole. A light Pinot Noir from Oregon, such as Adelsheim, or a slightly herbal one from Santa Barbara, California, such as Sanford, would carry all these flavors nicely. If you prefer the Burgundy route, go a bit south to the Côte Chalonnaise. The delicate, well-made Bourgogne by A. et P. de Villaine at Bouzeron will please.

Napoleon of Portobellas and Turnips with Ginger-Soy-Mirin Sauce

~~~~~~

Approximately 25 percent of my patrons order the vegetable tasting menu, which is really pretty incredible, considering that Charlie Trotter's is the furthest thing in the world from a vegetarian or health food restaurant. This mushroom preparation, with its somewhat Asian influence, has always met with great success. It never reminds you that you are "eating vegetarian," and that is really the highest goal when preparing vegetable dishes.

Serves 6

3 medium-large turnips

Vegetable Stock (optional) (see Appendix)

6 medium-sized portobella mushrooms

¼ cup dark sesame oil plus additional oil for the pan

1½ tablespoons soy sauce

Coriander sprigs

1½ teaspoons julienned ginger

Salt and pepper

Ginger-Soy-Mirin Sauce (recipe follows)

METHOD Peel the turnips and cover them with water or Vegetable Stock. Poach for 15 or 20 minutes until they are just barely cooked through. Cool them in the liquid. Cut the turnips into ¼-inch slices and set them aside. Remove the stems of the mushrooms and thoroughly clean the caps. Toss the mushroom caps with ¼ cup of sesame oil and the soy sauce; add the coriander sprigs and ginger, and mix thoroughly. Place in a roasting pan, cover with foil, and roast at 400 degrees for 20 to 30 minutes, until the mushrooms are thoroughly cooked. Cool the mushrooms. Line a 3 x 6 x 2-inch roasting pan with foil and lightly rub the foil with sesame oil. Arrange 2 of the portobella mushrooms on the bottom of the pan, slightly overlapping the edges, to create one flat, smooth layer. (You may need to trim the mushrooms and patch some spaces to form a solid layer.) Sprinkle on a little salt and pepper. Make a layer of turnips, trimming as necessary, lightly season, and then repeat until you have 3 layers of mushrooms and 3 layers of turnips. Cover with buttered foil. Set a second pan on top of the foil and weight it with a brick or other heavy, ovenproof object. Bake at 400 degrees for 30 to 40 minutes to thoroughly cook the mushrooms and turnips and to meld the flavors together. Cool at room temperature, still weighted, and refrigerate overnight still weighted. Drain off any excess liquid and reserve for the sauce. Cut into the desired shapes—round, square, etc. Just before serving, place on a roasting pan in a 400-degree oven for 10 to 15 minutes or until heated through.

ASSEMBLY Remove the napoleons from the oven onto 6 warm plates and spoon the sauce on and around them.

Ginger-Soy-Mirin Sauce

½ cup very tiny hon she meji mushroom caps

2 tablespoons sweet corn kernels

2 teaspoons peeled and finely minced ginger

1 tablespoon dark sesame oil

4 tablespoons rice vinegar

4 tablespoons mirin

4 tablespoons Vegetable Stock or Chicken Stock (see Appendix)

2 tablespoons soy sauce

1 tablespoon butter

2 teaspoons coriander leaves, cut into a fine chiffonade

Salt and pepper

METHOD In a medium-sized sauté pan, cook the mushrooms, corn, and ginger in the sesame oil over medium heat for 6 to 8 minutes to completely soften. Deglaze with rice vinegar and reduce to a glaze. Add the mirin, stock, soy sauce, and reserved mushroom-turnip liquid. Whisk in the butter, stir in the coriander, and season if necessary with salt and pepper.

Wine Notes

This Asian-inspired preparation is quite challenging. The intense herb, ginger, and pickling spice/vinegar flavors are very difficult for most wines because they are so sharp. Alsace comes to mind first, especially a heady Grand Cru Gewurztraminer, yet the mushrooms demand more body; and red wines seem completely at a loss to balance the dish. Perhaps the best solution is a fine Sake, served cold, because of its low acidity and because it echoes the mirin flavor.

Morel Flan with Black-Eyed Peas, Roasted Baby Fennel, and Herb-Infused Chicken Stock Reduction

Other than asparagus, there is no surer sign that spring has arrived than when the first morel mushrooms appear. This dish also features baby fennel and beautiful fresh black-eyed peas. In this earthy combination of early spring vegetables, everything supports the pungent, rich morel flavor. A delicate Herb-Infused Chicken Stock Reduction creates the perfect balance.

Serves 6

½ cup chopped, loosely packed, portobello mushrooms

3½ cups whole morel mushrooms, thoroughly cleaned

1 clove garlic, peeled and finely minced

1 shallot, peeled and finely minced

3 tablespoons plus 1 teaspoon unsalted butter

2 tablespoons water

1 egg plus 2 egg yolks

½ cup heavy cream

Salt and pepper

3 baby fennel bulbs

3 tablespoons olive oil

30 whole morel mushrooms, cleaned

6 tablespoons Chicken Stock (see Appendix)

Tarragon sprigs (reserve some for garnish)

1 cup fresh black-eyed peas, shelled

METHOD For the flan, place the portobello mushrooms and 3½ cups of morel mushrooms in a food processor and thoroughly purée. Sweat the garlic and shallot in 1 teaspoon of butter over medium heat until softened and translucent. Add the mushroom purée and water and cook, stirring frequently, until the mixture is thoroughly dry (about 15 to 18 minutes). Cool to room temperature. Lightly beat the egg with the egg yolks and thoroughly stir into the mushroom purée. Stir in the cream and season with salt and pepper. Butter 6 2-ounce molds with about 1 tablespoon of butter and fill with the flan mixture. Cook in a water bath at 350 degrees for about 40 minutes. A metal skewer inserted into the flan should emerge clean when the flan is cooked.

Toss the fennel in 1 tablespoon of olive oil and roast in a 400-degree oven for 8 to 10 minutes, or until the bulbs are completely cooked. Toss the 30 morel mushrooms in the remaining olive oil, 4 tablespoons of Chicken Stock, and the tarragon sprigs. Put this mixture in a roasting pan and cover with a lid or foil. Bake at 400 degrees for 15 minutes or so, until the mushrooms are cooked.

Blanch the black-eyed peas in boiling, salted water until they are just barely cooked (about 1 minute), then shock them in ice water.

Cut each fennel bulb lengthwise into 8 pieces. Melt 2 tablespoons of butter in a sauté pan and place the fennel in the pan. Add the whole morel mushrooms, black-eyed peas, and the remaining Chicken Stock. Braise everything for a minute or so and season with salt and pepper.

ASSEMBLY Arrange 4 pieces of baby fennel in the center of each plate. Spoon some of the black-eyed peas into the center, and arrange 5 morels on each plate in a star pattern. Place a flan on each mound of vegetables, and spoon 3 tablespoons of the reduction on each plate. Sprinkle on a few tarragon leaves.

Herb-Infused Chicken Stock Reduction

2 cups Chicken Stock (see Appendix)

2 or 3 basil leaves

2 or 3 tarragon sprigs

2 or 3 thyme sprigs

14 chives

3 to 4 lovage leaves

METHOD Slowly reduce the Chicken Stock by one-third to 1⅓ cups. Add the herbs and steep for 30 seconds and strain. (This sauce is quite thin, but that is by design.)

Wine Notes

Intensely rich and earthy, the concentration of the morel flavor in this dish is unforgettable. The inclusion of fennel adds another aromatic thrill. Both of these can be echoed by the same wine—a full-throttle, mountain-grown, peppery Cabernet Sauvignon from the Napa Valley, California, such as La Jota's or Philip Togni's. Other rather herbal Cabernets could also work, like Joseph Phelps's Backus Vineyard, or any of the Heitz Cabernets. If these wines seem too big, consider a softer style of Brunello di Montalcino, such as Banfi, which shows surprising suppleness and grace with this dish.

SALMON

—◆◆◆—

In my opinion, salmon is the most versatile fish of all, and I love it in every form. In fact, it is hard for me to get enough of it. I cure it, marinate it, smoke it, poach it, grill it, or roast it whole. It can be prepared with the skin on or off, served with meat or vegetable juices or with virtually no sauce at all. Although it is a relatively fatty fish, the high content of omega-3 fatty acids makes it as healthful as it is succulent. The fact that salmon can stand up to strong flavors opens up even more options. It lends itself beautifully to Pinot Noirs and soft Cabernets, especially when it is prepared with a meat reduction sauce or is accompanied by earthy elements such as mushrooms or certain root vegetables.

Salmon is always available in the restaurant, even when it is not on the printed menu, so I use it often for spontaneous, unannounced creations. Most of the salmon I serve is ocean-farmed off the coast of Maine, but when I am able to get it, I also use Columbia River salmon from the Pacific Northwest, and white salmon and Chinook from Alaska. Farmed Norwegian salmon is commonly available and would work perfectly well in the recipes that follow. Sturgeon or certain kinds of trout with a high fat content could be substituted in some of these dishes, too.

Smoked Salmon Terrine with Peeky Toe Crab and Parsley and Yellow Bell Pepper Juices

~~~~~~

I serve all manner of layered terrines at the restaurant as an alternative to heavy mousses or forcemeats. Not only are they lighter, but because the various components of the terrine are not puréed to a featureless whole, the flavor of each element is allowed to come through. In this particular terrine, an anchovy compound butter is spread lightly between the slices of smoked salmon, which gives the fish a slightly more intense flavor. You can substitute Foie Gras Butter (see Appendix), which will result in a richer terrine, or use an herb butter, which will make it more aromatic. This dish can be assembled in a variety of molds: just lay the spinach out in a rectangle the same length as the mold and 1½ times its circumference. For this recipe, I use a mold measuring 2 x 9 x 2½ inches, which will yield more than four servings, but it is difficult to make a smaller amount.

Serves 4

1½ to 2 pounds thinly sliced smoked salmon

½ cup butter, room temperature

2 ounces anchovies, rinsed and chopped

1 tablespoon lemon juice

1 shallot, finely minced

Salt and pepper

Grapeseed oil

½ pound spinach

Peeky Toe Crab Salad (recipe follows)

Corn Salad (recipe follows)

Parsley Juice (see Appendix)

Yellow Bell Pepper Juice (see Appendix)

METHOD Cut the salmon into 2-inch-wide pieces (or the width of your terrine). Using an electric mixer fitted with the paddle attachment, whip ½ cup of butter until it is thoroughly softened. Add the chopped anchovies, lemon juice, and minced shallots, and mix at medium speed for 30 to 40 seconds. Season to taste with salt and pepper. Reserve 2 to 3 tablespoons of the mixture. Rub the inside of a 2 x 9 x 2½-inch terrine mold with a little grapeseed oil and line it with plastic wrap. Put a layer of smoked salmon on the bottom of the mold and spread it with a very thin layer of anchovy butter. Continue to layer the salmon and butter until all the salmon is used up. Fold the plastic wrap over the fish and refrigerate for 2 to 3 hours to allow the butter to firm up.

In the meantime, clean and stem the spinach. Blanch the spinach in boiling water and shock it immediately in ice water, being careful to keep the leaves whole. It may be easier to do this in 3 or 4 batches. Drain and thoroughly blot off all the water with paper towels. On top of plastic wrap, lay out a rectangle of spinach measuring 14 x 9 inches. Carefully spread 2 to 3 tablespoons of the reserved anchovy butter over the spinach. When the terrine is set, remove it from the plastic, place it on the spinach (with the 9-inch side of the terrine along one 9-inch edge of the spinach), and roll it up, encasing it in the spinach and using the plastic wrap to help mold the spinach firmly around the terrine. Refrigerate until ready to serve.

ASSEMBLY Cut 4 ½-inch-thick slices of the terrine, and place a slice in the center of each plate. Place 3 or 4 mounds of Peeky Toe Crab Salad and 3 or 4 mounds of Corn Salad around each slice. Drizzle some of the Parsley Juice and Yellow Bell Pepper Juice onto each plate.

Peeky Toe Crab Salad

4 ounces Peeky Toe crab meat, cleaned (Dungeness and red rock crab also work well)

1½ teaspoons olive oil

1½ teaspoons finely chopped green onion

1½ teaspoons finely chopped red bell pepper

1 teaspoon snipped chives

Salt and pepper

METHOD Toss the crab with the olive oil, then add the remaining ingredients one by one, gently stirring after each one. Season with salt and pepper.

Corn Salad

¼ cup cooked corn kernels

¼ cup tomato concassée

2 tablespoons jicama, cut into a brunoise

1 teaspoon minced basil

1½ tablespoons olive oil or Herb Oil (see Appendix)

Salt and pepper

METHOD Toss together all the ingredients and season to taste with salt and pepper.

Wine Notes

A very dry yet complex and flavorful wine will succeed with this terrine. While the presence of shellfish and herbs and bell pepper leads one naturally to the Loire, even a pungent Pouilly-Fumé seems too light for the richness of the salmon, especially in this rendition. The ideal wine should be firm, dry, rich, and earthy. These attributes come together in Chablis, most notably in a barrel-fermented Chablis such as one of the fabulous Premier Cru wines of Raveneau. These sensual and challenging wines are worth the expense and the difficulty of finding them. Look for vineyards of Butteaux and Chapelot.

Timbale of Salmon Tartare with Osetra Caviar, Avocado, and Lemon Oil

Salmon plus caviar — together they form a sumptuous gastronomic combination that is bound to satisfy any food lover's fantasy. Each has its own opulent richness, such that in tandem, the two form a potent partnership. Here I add avocado for even more richness and then delicately cut into all the components with a touch of barely acidic lemon oil.

Serves 4

6 ounces salmon, finely diced

*4 tablespoons Lemon Oil
(must be made in advance; recipe follows)*

4 teaspoons snipped chives

1 tablespoon finely chopped shallot

Salt and pepper

1 to 3 ounces Osetra caviar (depending on how extravagant you want to be)

Pulped Avocado (recipe follows)

1 tablespoon cubed hard-boiled egg whites

2 teaspoons sieved hard-boiled egg yolk

1½ tablespoons tomato concassée

White pepper

METHOD Toss the salmon thoroughly with 1 tablespoon of Lemon Oil. Toss in 2 teaspoons of chives and the shallots and season to taste with salt and pepper. Keep refrigerated, or on ice, until ready to use.

ASSEMBLY Pack the salmon tartare into 4 small molds or cutters, and place a timbale in the center of each of 4 slightly chilled plates. Spoon the caviar onto the top of each timbale. Scoop 4 mounds of Pulped Avocado around each timbale, molding them into a quenelle shape if so desired. Sprinkle a little egg white and egg yolk around the timbales, add some tomato, and sprinkle on some of the chives. Drizzle 2 teaspoons of Lemon Oil around the edges of each plate and grind a small amount of white pepper on top.

Lemon Oil

Rind of 3 lemons

3 tablespoons lemon juice

1 cup minus 2 tablespoons grapeseed oil

2 tablespoons olive oil

½ teaspoon kosher salt

METHOD Combine all the ingredients in a blender and blend at high speed for 1½ minutes. Pour into a container and refrigerate for 2 or 3 days. Allow to stand at room temperature for 2 to 3 hours. Carefully decant the oil from the rind and juice through a cheesecloth. If desired, you could stir in a couple of teaspoons of finely grated lemon rind.

Pulped Avocado

1 avocado

1 tablespoon lemon juice

1 tablespoon tomato concassée

1 teaspoon snipped chives

Salt and pepper

METHOD Peel and pit the avocado. Mash it with a wooden spoon until well pulped. Add the lemon juice, tomato, and chives and mix thoroughly. Season to taste with salt and pepper.

Wine Notes

This early course, which combines the richness of salmon with the saltiness of aristocratic caviar, demands an elegant yet assertive wine. Champagne provides the acidity to counter the fatty salmon and avocado flavors, and its effervescence works famously with caviar. A heavier Brut or Blanc de Noirs style would create too much bitterness and tend to block out flavor. A lighter, Chardonnay-based Champagne, such as the luxury Comtes de Champagne Blanc de Blancs by Taittinger, will fit seamlessly and will also emphasize the delicate lemon hint at the finish.

Salmon Roulade with Anchovies, Ligurian Black Olive Sauce, Red Wine Reduction, and Saffron Oil

*There is nothing like anchovies and olives to give a lusty boost to the flavor of seafood.
In this particular preparation, the fattiness of the salmon is cut nicely by the salt in the olives
and anchovies, making the flavor of the fish even more explosive. A little drizzle
of the very intense Red Wine Reduction adds the final touch—just the right amount of
concentrated, complex acid to tie everything together flawlessly.*

Serves 4.

*4 skinless 4-ounce fillets of salmon,
cut lengthwise from a side*

1 tablespoon olive oil

1 teaspoon chopped tarragon

1 teaspoon chopped basil

Salt and pepper

*12 large spinach leaves, stemmed and
blanched*

12 small fillets oil-packed anchovy, rinsed

*12 strands Roasted Red Bell Pepper
(see Appendix)*

*4 tablespoons Ligurian Black Olive Sauce
(recipe follows)*

*2 tablespoons Red Wine Reduction
(see Appendix)*

4 teaspoons Saffron Oil (see Appendix)

4 teaspoons Parsley Juice (see Appendix)

METHOD Rub the salmon strips on all sides with olive oil, then rub on the chopped tarragon and basil, and finally a little salt and pepper. Roll the salmon strips into medium tight roulades with the former skin side outside and the thicker part of the salmon in the center of the roulade. Put the roulades in a nonstick pan, bake at 350 degrees for 4 to 5 minutes, then remove from the pan.

ASSEMBLY Place a roulade in the center of each plate. Arrange 3 pieces of blanched spinach, 3 anchovies, and 3 pieces of bell pepper around the roulade. Drizzle a little Ligurian Black Olive Sauce, Red Wine Reduction, Saffron Oil, and Parsley Juice around the edges of each plate.

Ligurian Black Olive Sauce

2 tablespoons Ligurian black olive paste
2 tablespoons Chicken Stock (see Appendix)

METHOD Whisk the Ligurian black olive paste and the Chicken Stock in a stainless-steel bowl over boiling water. Keep it warm until ready to serve.

Wine Notes

This visually stimulating dish also rewards the nose with the perfume of fragrant tarragon and saffron, with Provençal nuances of olive and anchovy. A fragrant wine will match up well with these elements. The salmon itself is light and feathery, so elegant that an overly oaky wine will interrupt its pleasure. While the ingredients on paper seem to call for red wine, only a dry white will preserve the delicacy of the fish while merging together all the flavors. A white from the south of France, like a young Mas de Daumas Gassac Blanc, can work, but an Hermitage Blanc from a traditional producer such as Chave or Sorrel will work wonders, especially if it has been cellared for several years. A mature Hermitage adds a nutty texture to the palate while elevating the components of the dish.

Salmon and Seared Foie Gras with Truffled Artichokes, Black Trumpet Mushrooms, and Tomato Water

*Both the foie gras and the salmon are quite rich, but this is cut perfectly by the
Tomato Water. The combination gains further depth with the addition of black trumpet mushrooms
and artichokes. When a little black truffle is added, the result is stunning.
This would be a glorious dish to include on a New Year's Eve menu.*

Serves 4

1 tablespoon grapeseed oil

1 8-ounce salmon fillet

Salt and pepper

4 1½-ounce slices foie gras, cleaned

1 artichoke heart, cooked and cut into small wedges

1 teaspoon finely julienned black truffles

1 teaspoon chopped parsley

1 cup black trumpet mushrooms, cleaned

1 cup Tomato Water (see Appendix)

METHOD Heat the grapeseed oil in a non-stick pan over medium-high heat and sear the salmon fillet on both sides, about 2 minutes total. (If the salmon fillet is very wide, cut the piece lengthwise down the pin bone line and proceed with 2 pieces.) Remove it from the pan and blot off excess oil. Season with salt and pepper and slice crosswise into 16 thin slices. Sear the foie gras over medium heat until each side is a rich, golden brown, but take care to leave the inside soft and pink. Remove to paper towels, thoroughly blot off excess fat, and season with salt and pepper. Reserve the rendered foie gras fat.

In a double boiler, warm the artichoke and truffle pieces in 2 teaspoons of foie gras fat. Season with salt and pepper and add the parsley. In a nonstick pan over medium heat, sauté the black trumpet mushrooms in about 1 tablespoon of the rendered foie gras fat until thoroughly cooked, about 4 to 5 minutes. Thoroughly blot the mushrooms and season with salt and pepper.

ASSEMBLY Arrange 4 slices of salmon in each bowl, and top with 1 piece of foie gras. Add the artichokes and truffles, and strew some of the mushrooms around the edges. Drizzle about ¼ cup of Tomato Water on each serving.

Wine Notes

The exciting, hedonistic pleasure of this dish will be amplified by a wine of some rich sweetness for the foie gras as well as some tartness to balance the meaty salmon. The salty and tart Tomato Water does some of the job, yet opens the possibility for a sweeter wine. A great Vouvray from a ripe vintage will be a thrilling choice, such as Prince Poniatowski's Clos Baudoin 1989.

However, if you prefer to accentuate the earthy flavors of the truffles and the black mushrooms, there is no better wine for this purpose than a mature red Burgundy. This type of wine is certainly appropriate for the foie gras and salmon combination, especially if the dish is used as a main course. A mature Clos de Tart or a rich Bonnes-Mares from Comte de Vogüé will make a splendid and memorable flavor experience.

Salmon with Olympia Oysters, Hijiki Seaweed, and Ginger-Shiso-Mirin Broth

There is nothing like the crispy seared skin of salmon to augment the rich flavor of the meat. This preparation is made particularly appealing by the luscious little Olympia oysters from Washington State. The exotic-tasting broth, accented by the shiso and the ginger, allows the beautiful flavors of the salmon and the oysters to shine through. The hijiki seaweed adds a wonderful crunchy contrast to the silky oysters. A little bread may be appropriate to sop up every bit of sauce!

Serves 4

1 tablespoon dried hijiki seaweed

2 teaspoons grapeseed oil

4 2-ounce salmon pieces, skin on

Salt and pepper

2 tablespoons butter

½ cup leeks, cut into rings

1 tablespoon Preserved Ginger (see Appendix)

1 tablespoon rice vinegar

3 tablespoons mirin

⅔ cup Fish Stock (see Appendix)

32 Olympia oysters

½ tablespoon shiso

METHOD Soak the hijiki seaweed in cold water for 20 minutes. Drain and set aside. In a medium sauté pan, heat the grapeseed oil over medium-high heat. Slit the skin on the top of the salmon to prevent the salmon from buckling. Sauté the salmon, skin side down, for 1½ minutes. Turn and cook for 30 seconds or so. Season with salt and pepper and remove to a warm place. In the same pan, melt 1 tablespoon of butter, add the leeks, and turn the heat down to medium. Stew the leeks for 2 minutes or so until they soften. Add the Preserved Ginger and deglaze with rice vinegar. Add the mirin and Fish Stock, bring to a boil, and remove from heat. Stir in the hijiki seaweed and the oysters, and allow the oysters to just warm through. Add the shiso, whisk in the remaining tablespoon of butter, and season to taste with salt and pepper.

ASSEMBLY Spoon the oysters and leeks evenly into 4 warm bowls, place a piece of salmon on top, and spoon in the broth.

Wine Notes

This exotic and aromatic preparation of salmon adds so many Asian spices and flavors that only a vibrant and floral white wine will do. American Gewurztraminer comes to mind, but many versions of this variety may seem bitter, so one must choose carefully. Navarro, from the Anderson Valley of Northern California, will be a reliable tablemate. Viognier will also match the fragrances of the dish, and a high-toned wine like the Arrowood or the more austere Alban will make a nice foil as well.

Poached Salmon with Lobster Potatoes and Veal Stock Reduction

Without a doubt, one of the best ways to enjoy salmon is simply to poach it.
The elegance of the fish becomes apparent with this particular cooking technique,
especially in a preparation such as this in which the salmon is combined with chunks
of lobster meat, hearty potatoes, and a rich Veal Stock Reduction.

Serves 4

1 head garlic, cut in half

1 onion, peeled and coarsely chopped

1 fennel bulb, coarsely chopped

1 leek, coarsely chopped

1 orange, coarsely chopped

1 red bell pepper, cored, seeded and coarsely chopped

½ cup plus 6 tablespoons butter

2 cups high-quality Chardonnay

3 cups water

4 bay leaves

Salt and white pepper

1 large Idaho potato, unpeeled

2 tablespoons crème fraîche (or heavy cream)

⅔ cup cooked, chopped lobster meat

2 tablespoons crispy bacon pieces

2 teaspoons chopped parsley

Black pepper

4 3-ounce skinless salmon fillets

½ cup Veal Stock Reduction (see Appendix)

2 teaspoons finely julienned tarragon

METHOD To make a poaching liquid, sweat the garlic, onion, fennel, leek, orange, and bell pepper in ½ cup of butter until thoroughly softened. Add the wine, water, and bay leaves and simmer for 20 minutes. Strain, discarding the solids, and season with salt and white pepper.

Boil the potato until soft and pass through a food mill. While still hot, whisk in the remaining 6 tablespoons of butter bit by bit, allowing each bit to melt before adding more. Whisk in the crème fraîche, then fold in the lobster meat, bacon, and parsley. Season with salt and pepper. Keep warm over a double boiler but do not hold for more than 15 minutes, or the lobster meat will become chewy.

Heat the poaching liquid to a simmer in a pan wide enough to allow the 4 salmon fillets to be completely submerged. Poach the fillets for approximately 3 minutes, turning them over once, halfway through cooking. Slightly more or less cooking time may be required depending on the thickness of the pieces of fish. Ideally, the fish should be cooked to a perfect medium-rare.

Remove and season lightly on both sides with salt and pepper. The poaching liquid can be reused or reduced for use in a sauce. Heat the Veal Stock Reduction.

ASSEMBLY Place a large dollop of lobster potatoes in the center of each plate, and top each mound with a salmon fillet. Drizzle 2 tablespoons of Veal Stock Reduction around the potatoes, and garnish the salmon with the julienned tarragon.

Wine Notes

The lobster potatoes add a hearty, rich flavor to this dish, while the poached salmon retains its sea freshness, so a rich California Chardonnay should put it all together. The always sensuous Kistler *Dutton Ranch* Chardonnay is smoky from dark-toasted oak, matching the sweetness of the lobster while standing up to the richness of the stock reduction. Other excellent full-bodied Chardonnays that will work include the Newton *Unfiltered* and the Talbott *Diamond T Estate*.

SCALLOPS

For the last six years, I have been using *diver* scallops from Maine almost
exclusively. These sea scallops are hand-harvested by scuba divers; they are
plucked off the rocks one by one, and shipped live in the shell. There is a
world of difference between these scallops and those that are net-harvested.
In net harvesting, the shells break up and pierce the meat, so that much of
the flavor bleeds off into the sea. Furthermore, the meat becomes pulverized
and bruised, so that when the scallop is placed in the pan, it literally steams
in what is left of its juices. Diver scallops, on the other hand, are as firm as a
piece of steak, retain all their rich flavor, and caramelize beautifully because
their juices are still intact. There is simply no comparison in flavor or
texture. The recipes that follow would work with ordinary sea scallops, but
it would easily be worth the trouble and expense to try to obtain these incredible diver scallops.

Scallops require little preparation but they should be cleaned and the tough
muscle attaching them to the shell must be removed. I like to work with
scallops because their possibilities are almost unlimited. They can be eaten
raw or cooked; marinated or smoked. I've even braised scallops in meat
juices with incredible results. They are wonderful in very unpretentious
preparations where they are simply sautéed and accompanied by a straightforward sauce. On the other hand, they lend themselves to very complicated
treatments, too. They also take well to a variety of flavorings, from very
pungent horseradish, to the exotic Asian spices, to the subtle flavors of basil
and chervil.

Marinated Scallops with Horseradish Potatoes, Mustard Oil, and Parsley Juice

~~~~~~

The natural sweetness of sea scallops benefits tremendously from a little heat:
in this preparation, it comes in the form of horseradish and mustard. First, diced potatoes
are poached and tossed in a horseradish mayonnaise sauce for a potato salad effect.
Then a touch of Mustard Oil adds another accent of measured heat that perfectly harmonizes
with the raw, clear sharpness of the horseradish. The Crispy Potato Rings create
a textural contrast that is essential to the success of this dish.

Serves 4

*4 2-to-2½-ounce hand-harvested
sea scallops*

Juice of 1 lemon

1 tablespoon olive oil

1 tablespoon grapeseed oil

1 tablespoon chopped parsley

Salt and pepper

32 to 40 paper-thin slices of cucumber

4 Crispy Potato Rings (recipe follows)

*1½ cups Horseradish Potatoes
(recipe follows)*

Red Bell Pepper Juice (see Appendix)

Mustard Oil (recipe follows)

Parsley Juice (see Appendix)

Fennel fronds or chervil for garnish

METHOD Cut each scallop into 6 to 8 thin slices. Whisk together the lemon juice, olive oil, grapeseed oil, chopped parsley, and a pinch of salt and pepper. Rub the slices thoroughly with the marinade and refrigerate 4 hours before serving.

ASSEMBLY Fan a few cucumber slices in the center of each plate and top with a Crispy Potato Ring. Fill each ring with Horseradish Potatoes. Form a pinwheel of scallops above the potatoes. Drizzle the Bell Pepper Juice, Mustard Oil, and Parsley Juice onto each plate and garnish with fennel or chervil.

Horseradish Potatoes

1 large potato

1½ teaspoons Dijon mustard

1 small egg yolk

6 tablespoons grapeseed oil

1½ teaspoons lemon juice

½ cup grated horseradish

Salt and pepper

1½ teaspoons chopped parsley

1 tablespoon finely sliced red onion

METHOD Peel the potato and cut it into a ⅛-inch dice. Poach until al dente, drain, and set aside to cool. Little by little, whisk the mustard into the egg yolk, then whisk in the grapeseed oil to form a mayonnaise. Whisk in the lemon juice and add the horseradish. Season to taste with salt and pepper. Fold in the potatoes, parsley, and red onion.

Crispy Potato Rings

2 large potatoes

Grapeseed oil

Salt and pepper

METHOD Peel and trim the potatoes in rectangles and cut lengthwise into ⅛-inch slices. Line a sheet pan with parchment paper and rub on a little grapeseed oil. Make 4 rows of potatoes, using 3 or 4 slices of potato per row, with each slice slightly overlapping the last (each row needs to be long enough to encircle a 2½-inch pastry ring). Oil a second piece of parchment paper and place it oiled side down over the potatoes. Top with another sheet pan and place an ovenproof weight on the pan. Bake at 500 degrees for 4 minutes and allow to cool, still weighted, for 3 minutes. Lightly oil 4 2½-inch pastry rings and wrap each with a ring of potato slices. Bake at 350 degrees for 5 to 10 minutes or until they are crispy and golden brown. Immediately remove the pastry rings or they will stick. Season with salt and pepper.

Mustard Oil

¼ cup mustard seed

¼ cup grapeseed oil

*1 teaspoon dried mustard reconstituted in
1 tablespoon water*

1 teaspoon turmeric

METHOD Roast the mustard seed in a sauté pan. Allow to cool and blend vigorously with the grapeseed oil, mustard, and turmeric. Pour into a container, cover, and refrigerate. Allow to settle for 24 hours and slowly decant the oil through a fine mesh sieve.

Wine Notes

The slightly hot elements of this dish would be exaggerated by a wine with a higher degree of alcohol, so choose a cool-climate, fruity white that refreshes and still preserves the scallop sweetness. A light Pinot Blanc from Alsace, like the Zind-Humbrecht Pinot d'Alsace or the Hugel *Cuvée les Amours* will merge with these flavors beautifully. If you prefer to make the horseradish and mustard themes stand out, then a crisp Blanc de Blancs Champagne will be useful. Or if you would like to experiment with a wine seldom seen in the American market, a Swiss Dezaley l'Arbalete would be an eye-opening experience.

Scallops with Pickled Lamb's Tongue and Truffled Celery Broth

I first prepared this dish in January 1993 at the James Beard House in New York in a collaboration dinner with Chef David Bouley that featured varietal meats. Since then I have developed a number of variations on this theme. The scallops are rich and so is the lamb's tongue, but between the clean, sure Celery Broth and the delicate acid from the pickled tongue, there is a perfect balance of complex flavors. The black trumpet mushrooms and the white truffle oil provide the dish with the final, perfect element of luxury. Also intriguing is the balance of full-flavored lusciousness, even earthiness, juxtaposed — primarily because of the broth — with wholesome lightness.

Serves 4

2 ½ tablespoons unsalted butter

4 large hand-harvested sea scallops

Salt and pepper

4 long, thin slices zucchini

⅔ cup black trumpet mushrooms

2 Pickled Lamb's Tongues (see Appendix)

1 cup Celery Broth (recipe follows)

8 teaspoons white truffle oil

METHOD In a medium sauté pan, melt 1 tablespoon of butter over medium heat and sauté the scallops until they are just medium-rare, about 1 minute on each side. Remove them to a warm place and season with salt and pepper.

Melt ½ tablespoon of butter and brush the zucchini slices on both sides. Lightly season with salt and pepper. Lay the slices on a foil- or parchment-lined roasting pan and roast for 3 minutes in a 400-degree oven.

Thoroughly clean the mushrooms through repeated rinsing in cold water. In a medium sauté pan, melt the remaining tablespoon of butter and, stirring frequently, lightly sauté the mushrooms over medium-high heat for 3 to 4 minutes until thoroughly cooked. Season with salt and pepper, place on paper towels, and remove to a warm spot. Cut each lamb's tongue into 4 lengthwise slices and place in a 400-degree oven for 2 minutes to warm. Slice each of the scallops into thirds.

ASSEMBLY Put a mound of black trumpet mushrooms in the center of each bowl. Place a slice of scallop, a slice of lamb's tongue, another slice of scallop, and another slice of tongue on top of the mushrooms. Top with a folded slice of zucchini, then crown this small pyramid with a final slice of scallop. Pour ¼ cup or so of hot Celery Broth in each bowl and drizzle about 2 teaspoons of white truffle oil into the broth. It will bead and float and create a glorious effect. (This dish also works quite well when the scallops and tongue are grilled. The layering can be done in any fashion you wish. Indeed, the ingredients do not need to be layered at all, but could simply be tossed together.)

Celery Broth

3 cups Celery Juice (see Appendix)

1 small celery root, peeled and cut up

Salt and pepper

METHOD Place the Celery Juice and celery root in a saucepan and bring to a boil. The Celery Juice will separate, so it is important to thoroughly skim the resulting foam and particles as they appear. Simmer for 45 minutes, then strain through a fine strainer lined with cheesecloth. Continue to simmer until reduced by one-third. Season with salt and pepper. Reheat before serving.

Wine Notes

This preparation could take many tacks as far as the wine accompaniment goes. The rich scallop needs a round, buttery, rich Chardonnay, yet the lamb's tongue is so meaty and sharply flavored that only a red wine, and a rather hefty one like Brunello or Bordeaux, will do. However, the Celery Broth tips the dish in the white direction. A version of this dish was served at the restaurant for the unveiling of the fabulous Matanzas Creek *Journey* Chardonnay 1990, and the two in tandem provided a stunning flavor experience. Many other full-bodied Chardonnays could fit in as well, including Talbott, Calera, or a mature Grgich Hills.

Sea Scallops with Braised Turnips, Watercress, Preserved Ginger, and Beet Juice

~~~~~~

The earthy sweetness of the Beet Juice provides just the right balance for the luscious scallops.
The Preserved Ginger and the watercress, respectively, add exotic and peppery qualities
that give this preparation a poetic Asian cast. There is the slightest bit of crunch to the leeks,
just enough to add an engaging bit of textural contrast to the soft scallops.

Serves 4

1 tablespoon grapeseed oil

1 tablespoon butter

Salt and pepper

4 2-to-2½-ounce sea scallops

1½ bunches watercress

¼ cup julienned leeks
(they can also be cut into rings)

½ tablespoon Preserved Ginger
(see Appendix)

Beet Juice (see Appendix)

Braised Turnips (recipe follows)

METHOD Heat a heavy-bottomed sauté pan to a medium-high heat. Add the grapeseed oil and butter and quickly place all of the scallops in the pan. After about 1 minute, flip them over and continue to cook for another minute. Remove the scallops from the pan, season with salt and pepper, and set aside in a warm spot. Add the watercress to the pan, which should have a little of the scallop juice in it, and lightly wilt for about 40 seconds. Sprinkle with salt and pepper and remove from pan. Poach the julienned leeks in boiling water until wilted but still slightly crunchy, and toss them with the Preserved Ginger. Season to taste with salt and pepper. Warm the Beet Juice.

ASSEMBLY Place 2 or 3 slices of warm braised turnips on each plate, and distribute the watercress evenly on top of the turnips. Place a scallop on each mound of watercress and top with leeks. Drizzle warm Beet Juice around the plate.

Braised Turnips

1 medium carrot, peeled and diced

1 medium onion, peeled and diced

1 medium stalk celery, peeled and diced

1 tablespoon bacon fat

2 medium turnips, peeled

1½ quarts Chicken Stock (see Appendix)

METHOD Sweat the carrot, onion, and celery in the bacon fat, stirring frequently until golden brown. Add the turnips and Chicken Stock and braise over medium heat for 40 minutes or so until thoroughly cooked. The braising liquid can be saved for a tremendous soup.

Wine Notes

This striking dish needs a wine that will stand up to the intensity of the ginger and root vegetables, while delicately allowing the scallop's creaminess to fill the palate. Alsace provides the right wine as it so often does—a fine, young Gewurztraminer from a lighter producer like Josmeyer will be heady enough to work with the earthy components and elegant enough to push the scallop flavor forward.

Scallop Ceviche with Seaweed, Asian Vegetables, and Coriander Water

~~~~~~

*I consider this to be the ultimate health food. It is so clean, light, and full of flavor that consuming
it makes you feel as though you have done something good for your body. It is crucial to the dish that the various
types of seaweed used in it be fresh. Do not used dried or preserved seaweed. If the particular varieties
called for are not available at your Asian market, look for a high-quality premixed seaweed mixture.
The crunchy texture of the seaweed along with the vegetables and scallops makes for a delicate complexity.
Finally, I love the explosive, pure flavor of the Coriander Water in this cool, refreshing dish.*

Serves 4

6 2-to-2 ½-ounce hand-harvested sea scallops

1 tablespoon rice vinegar

1 tablespoon lime juice

1 tablespoon orange juice

1 tablespoon Fish Stock (see Appendix)

½ tablespoon coriander leaves

1 tablespoon dark sesame oil

½ cup boiled cellophane noodles

2 tablespoons limu ogo, rinsed and chopped

2 tablespoons agar-agar, rinsed and chopped

2 tablespoons kelp, rinsed and chopped

¼ cup julienned daikon

¼ cup julienned and poached leeks

¼ cup Napa cabbage, cut into a fine chiffonade

2 teaspoons finely julienned squash blossoms

1 tablespoon ponzu sauce

Coriander Water (recipe follows)

METHOD Cut each scallop into 4 pieces and toss together with the rice vinegar, lime juice, orange juice, Fish Stock, coriander leaves, and sesame oil. Marinate for 2 to 3 hours in the refrigerator.

Carefully toss together the noodles, limu ogo, agar-agar, kelp, daikon, poached leeks, Napa cabbage, squash blossoms, and ponzu sauce.

Toss everything together just before serving.

ASSEMBLY Distribute the ceviche among 4 bowls and add about 3 tablespoons of chilled Coriander Water to each.

Coriander Water

2 bunches coriander leaves, blanched and shocked in ice water

¼ to 1 cup water

1 teaspoon salt

METHOD Purée all ingredients and pour through a coffee filter. It may take 20 or 30 minutes to drip through. Chill until used.

Wine Notes

The tartness of the marinade and the bright herbal flash of coriander demand a crisp, high-acid wine that will also support the sweetness of the scallop and the elegance of the Asian ingredients. The cool-climate Friulian white wines of Puiatti offer a range of possibilities, but the best match is the Pinot Bianco. This crisp, clean wine does not convey the slight tropical tones often expressed by this variety, and therefore allows all the complex flavors of the dish to shine through.

Bay Scallops with Braised Celery, Red Wine Reduction, and Celery Oil

~~~~~~

Bay scallops right out of the shell are so sweet they taste like candy. I prefer the scallops from Nantucket Sound, but any fresh bay scallop can be substituted. In this preparation I have balanced that sweetness with aromatic celery and a concentrated, full-flavored Red Wine Reduction. A few roasted bell pepper pieces enhance the sweetness of the scallops, and the Celery Oil ties all the elements together with a playful richness.

Serves 4

50 to 60 bay scallops, freshly removed from their shells (about 3 pounds)

3 tablespoons butter

Salt and pepper

¼ cup Chicken Stock (see Appendix)

2 stalks celery, peeled and sliced

2 tablespoons Roasted Red Bell Pepper, chopped (see Appendix)

2 tablespoons cooked adzuki beans (or black beans)

½ cup Red Wine Reduction (see Appendix)

1 teaspoon snipped chives

2 tablespoons Celery Oil (recipe follows)

METHOD In a large sauté pan, melt 2 tablespoons of butter over medium-high heat, and sauté the scallops for 2 minutes or so (it is imperative to keep the scallops slightly underdone). Season with salt and pepper and remove to a warm spot. Heat the Chicken Stock in a small pan and add the remaining tablespoon of butter and the sliced celery. Braise the celery over medium-low heat for 4 to 5 minutes and strain off the liquid. Season with salt and pepper and keep warm. Warm the bell pepper pieces and the beans. Warm the Red Wine Reduction.

ASSEMBLY Spoon about 2 tablespoons of the Red Wine Reduction onto each plate. Put the celery on the center of the plates and mound the scallops on top. Add the bell peppers and beans and sprinkle on a few chives. Drizzle 1 or 2 tablespoons of Celery Oil around the edges of each plate.

Celery Oil

1 cup packed celery leaves

½ cup grapeseed oil

1 tablespoon olive oil

Salt and pepper

METHOD Thoroughly rinse the celery leaves and blanch for 5 seconds, then shock them in ice water. In a blender, blend the celery leaves, grapeseed oil, and olive oil on high speed for 45 seconds or so. Season with salt and pepper and strain through a fine strainer.

Wine Notes

The sweet red bell pepper and bay scallop flavors would be handsomely offset by a surprising choice—a light Rosé from southern France. The Domaine Tempier Bandol Rosé is a fresh, crisp, dry, yet fruity counterpoint to the components that make this dish so attractive. Other useful Rosés come from Domaine de Triennes and the Sancerre-Chavignol by Cotat.

Pinwheel of Scallops with
Summer Vegetables and Scallop Roe Broth

In this preparation, the scallops are thinly sliced and briefly sautéed,
which allows for maximum caramelization, and thus for maximum sweetness. The broth is
nothing more than Tomato Water blended together with the roe of the scallop to give it
a decided of-the-sea scallop flavor. It is reminiscent of the flavor of a mussel but much more
concentrated. A good seafood merchant can get scallops with the roe still attached.
I use an assortment of summer vegetables as the bridge between the broth and the unctuous scallop
meat, though you can certainly substitute other vegetables — asparagus, peas, snow peas,
or artichokes, for instance. Let the seasons be your guide.

Serves 4

4 jumbo hand-harvested sea scallops,
roe reserved for the sauce

2 to 3 tablespoons grapeseed oil

5 tablespoons unsalted butter

20 haricots verts, cut on a bias into
1-inch pieces

12 tiny yellow squash, quartered

8 tiny zucchini, cut on a bias into pieces

6 to 8 fresh green beans, cut on a bias
into pieces

2 teaspoons fennel fronds, finely chopped
(or dill or any other desired herb)

Salt and pepper

1 cup Scallop Roe Broth (recipe follows)

METHOD Cut each scallop into 6 or 7 slices. Cut 4 4-inch-square pieces of parchment paper, and rub a little grapeseed oil on one side only of each. Fan the scallop slices to create 4 *pinwheels*, and place each one on a parchment square. In a large nonstick pan, heat 1 tablespoon of grapeseed oil and 1 tablespoon of butter over medium-high heat. Place 2 of the pinwheels, scallop side down, in the pan. Cook for about 45 seconds, lift off the parchment (the scallops should now stick together), and continue to cook for another 45 seconds. Carefully remove them from the pan with a spatula and put them, cooked side up, in a warm spot. They will continue to cook to the right degree of doneness. Repeat the process with the other 2 pinwheels. Season all of them lightly with salt and pepper.

In another large sauté pan, sauté the vegetables in the remaining 4 tablespoons butter over medium-high heat until they just begin to brown and are thoroughly cooked. Season with salt and pepper, toss in the fennel fronds, and remove to a paper towel in a warm place.

ASSEMBLY Distribute the sautéed vegetables among 4 warm bowls. Place a pinwheel in the center of each bowl and pour in a little broth.

Scallop Roe Broth

1 cup Tomato Water (see Appendix)

Reserved scallop roe
4 tablespoons butter, softened
Salt and pepper

METHOD Just before serving, bring the Tomato Water to a boil. Remove from heat and add the roe to warm slightly. Pour the Tomato Water and roe into a blender and blend at medium-high speed for 30 to 45 seconds, adding the butter bit by bit into the running blender. Season to taste with salt and pepper. Pass through a fine strainer. Do not reheat this sauce — it must be prepared at the last minute.

Wine Notes

This dish will be enhanced by a lighter style of Chardonnay that sees no oak. Jean-Marie Guffens, who makes splendid Pouilly-Fuissé in Mâcon, also oversees the wines of Verget, a negotiant. Verget's St.-Véran is a fresh, lively expression of Chardonnay, and would serve this delicately flavored, somewhat sweet dish well.

TUNA

I love bigeye and bluefin tuna, both of which have a relatively high fat content, and are therefore especially good for raw preparations. Yellowfin tuna is somewhat less oily, but can still be used in all the following recipes with excellent results. It is the most readily available type of fresh tuna. For all my preparations, I use the highest grade of tuna, sashimi-grade. For many of the dishes, I trim the loins to yield neat small square shapes, which can be expensive, but I believe is well worth it, in terms of aesthetics. Besides, scraps can easily be turned into tartare for a great treat.

Tuna is so wonderful raw that in most of my preparations, I simply sear it briefly, leaving it uncooked on the inside. When I do cook tuna, I treat it as I would a fine steak—searing it on the outside, and leaving it rare in the middle (I never cook tuna past rare unless I am specifically requested to do so). Because it is so rich, tuna can stand up to a fair amount of spice and heat, and lends itself well to preparations with curry, horseradish, ginger, and chiles. I also love to pair it with the unusual or unlikely, such as lamb's tongue or blood sausage.

I think that tuna is the finest fish of all for the wine connoisseur, because it stands up well to everything from a Sake or Champagne to the richest of full-bodied reds.

Tuna-Wrapped Oysters with Saffron-Infused Tomato Water

I have prepared several versions of this dish, but this one is my favorite. The exotically perfumed Saffron-Infused Tomato Water ties together the flavors of rich tuna and the buttery oysters, while the small pieces of apple add just the right textural balance, as well as an intriguing bit of sweetness. The dish is cool and refreshing—perfect for late summer.

Serves 4

20 small oysters (e.g., Quilscenes or Fanny Bays)

20 chervil sprigs

20 paper-thin slices of tuna

½ English cucumber, very thinly sliced

20 or so saffron threads, roasted in a pan for a few seconds

1 tablespoon Preserved Ginger (see Appendix)

1 cup Saffron-Infused Tomato Water (recipe follows)

30 or 40 Parisienne balls of Red Delicious or Granny Smith apple

METHOD Shuck the oysters. Place a sprig of chervil on each oyster and wrap the oyster with a slice of tuna.

ASSEMBLY Place 5 small mounds of sliced cucumber in each bowl and top each with a tuna-wrapped oyster. Garnish each oyster with 1 or 2 saffron threads and 1 or 2 strands of ginger. Pour ¼ cup of chilled Saffron-Infused Tomato Water into each bowl and garnish with the apples.

Saffron-Infused Tomato Water

1 cup Tomato Water (see Appendix)
2 saffron threads

METHOD Bring the Tomato Water to a boil and steep the saffron threads in the water for a minute or so. Strain, cool, and then decant away any remaining sediment. Chill before serving.

Wine Notes

The rare, meaty tuna in this dish carries a number of balanced, delicate flavors: salty marine oysters, pungent saffron, and spicy ginger. All these components come together with a full-bodied sparkling wine. The great Champagnes of Krug are a regal accompaniment, but the flavors of Veuve Clicquot's Gold Label also work well with the Tomato Water. For greater fruit emphasis, try a New World Rosé. One of the best is from Iron Horse in Sonoma County, California.

Tuna Loin and Potato-Wrapped Beef Tenderloin with Horseradish Oil and Bell Pepper Juices

~~~~~~

From time to time I pair meat and fish, using just the smallest amount of spice or heat to bind the two together. In this dish, for example, the horseradish cuts nicely into both the tuna and the beef, highlighting their similarities. The fact that the texture of tuna is quite close to that of beef is particularly emphasized in this preparation. Swordfish and beef would also be a seamless match.

Serves 4

3 tablespoons grapeseed oil

4 tablespoons unsalted butter

8 ounces beef tenderloin, trimmed to 1½- to 2-inch diameter

15 to 20 spinach leaves, cleaned and stemmed

1 potato, peeled and very thinly sliced lengthwise

8 ounces tuna loin, trimmed to 1½- to 2-inch diameter

3 medium shallots, peeled and cut into fine rings

Flour

2 cups grapeseed oil for frying shallots

Salt and pepper

Horseradish Oil (recipe follows)

Red Bell Pepper Juice (see Appendix)

Yellow Bell Pepper Juice (see Appendix)

METHOD Heat 1 tablespoon of grapeseed oil and 1 tablespoon of butter in a medium sauté pan over medium-high heat, and sear the beef tenderloin on all sides. Remove from heat and allow to cool. Blanch the spinach in boiling water and shock it immediately in ice water, being careful to keep the leaves whole. It may be easier to do this in 3 or 4 batches. Drain and thoroughly blot off all the water with paper towels. On a piece of plastic wrap, lay out the spinach leaves to form a rectangle large enough to completely encase the meat. Roll up the beef tenderloin in the spinach, using the plastic wrap to help mold the spinach firmly around the meat. Refrigerate for 20 minutes or so. In the meantime, melt 1 tablespoon of butter, brush it on the potato slices, and lay them out on parchment paper. Bake at 350 degrees for 4 to 5 minutes until just softened. Cool to room temperature, and lay them out on plastic wrap in a rectangle (like the spinach). Carefully remove the plastic wrap from the spinach-wrapped beef and roll it up in the potato, again using the plastic wrap to help make it quite tight. Refrigerate for at least 1 hour.

Shortly before serving, carefully remove the plastic wrap from the beef and lightly season with salt and pepper. Heat 1 tablespoon of butter and 1 tablespoon of grapeseed oil in a medium sauté pan over medium-high heat, and sauté the beef on all sides until the potato is golden brown, about 6 to 8 minutes in all. The meat should still be quite rare. Remove to a warm spot. Heat 1 tablespoon of grapeseed oil and 1 tablespoon of butter, and sauté the tuna over medium-high heat on all sides, about 4 to 5 minutes total. It should be warmed through but still quite rare. Remove to paper towels and season with salt and pepper. Toss the shallots in flour, fry in grapeseed oil until golden brown, and remove to a paper towel. Slice the potato-wrapped beef into 12 or so thin slices. Do the same with the tuna.

ASSEMBLY For each serving, alternate 3 slices of beef with 3 slices of tuna in a rough pinwheel. Place a small mound of fried shallots on top of each pinwheel. Drizzle a little Horseradish Oil and the two bell pepper juices onto each plate.

Horseradish Oil

1 cup freshly grated horseradish

1 cup grapeseed oil

2 tablespoons rice vinegar

1 teaspoon salt

1 teaspoon ground pepper

METHOD Put all the ingredients in a blender and purée. Refrigerate for at least 1 day. Straining is optional. For this preparation I leave in much of the horseradish pulp because I like the texture.

Wine Notes

The sweet elements of caramelized shallot, along with the sweet bell pepper juices, help bridge the flavors of a rich, ripe Merlot with this meaty dish. The zesty pop of horseradish can be tamed by a fairly extracted Merlot by any number of California producers. Joe Cafaro, a Napa Valley winemaker and consultant, crafts a wine that will work well with its silky fullness. Dick Arrowood makes intense Merlot from Sonoma fruit. Better-known, larger producers, such as Duckhorn and Matanzas Creek, also make signature wines with this versatile variety.

Seared Raw Tuna with Chanterelle Mushrooms, French Green Lentils, and Veal Stock Reduction

Tuna is so rich and full-flavored that it stands up well to earthy, rustic components such as lentils and chanterelle mushrooms. I use French green lentils because they have a great flavor and they keep their shape after cooking. In this particular dish, the reduced Veal Stock adds a heartiness that really binds together the remaining ingredients.

Serves 4

2 teaspoons grapeseed oil

4 tablespoons unsalted butter

1 8- to 12-ounce tuna loin

Salt and pepper

2 cups chanterelle mushrooms, cleaned and most of the stem removed

2 teaspoons snipped chives

½ cup cooked French green lentils

1 tablespoon each carrot, bell pepper, and zucchini, cut into a brunoise

½ cup Veal Stock Reduction (see Appendix)

METHOD Heat the grapeseed oil and 1 tablespoon of butter in a medium sauté pan over medium-high heat, and sear the tuna on all sides. The whole process should take no more than 2 minutes. Remove the tuna from the pan to a warm spot and lightly season with salt and pepper.

Heat 2 tablespoons of butter in a medium sauté pan over medium heat and sauté the mushrooms for 5 or 6 minutes or until they are well cooked. They should be stirred from time to time. When they are done, toss in the chives and season with salt and pepper. Remove from the pan and keep in a warm place. Sauté the lentils and the vegetables in the remaining tablespoon of butter over medium heat for 2 to 3 minutes, stirring constantly. Remove them to a paper towel to thoroughly blot.

ASSEMBLY Spoon the mushrooms onto the center of each plate. Thinly slice the tuna into 20 or more pieces and carefully fan out 5 or 6 pieces on top of each bed of mushrooms. Spoon the lentil-vegetable mixture around the mushrooms and drizzle 2 or 3 tablespoons of Veal Stock Reduction onto each plate.

Wine Notes

This preparation combines the fresh ocean flavors of tuna with the earthy flavors of mushrooms and lentils, all bound together by a light meat reduction. The wine that makes the most sense here should be hearty enough for meat, yet subtle enough for the peppery spiciness of the dish; firm and structured, but not overwhelming. Burgundy, of course, comes to mind easily, especially in a full, ripe vintage such as 1990. Try a big Pommard from Domaine de Courcel for a thrilling treat. A number of modern California Zinfandels also work well, including Storybook Mountain, Nalle, and Quivera.

Peppered Tuna with Red Wine-Wild Mushroom-Foie Gras Broth and Potato Gnocchi

*This dish has two rich components, the tuna itself and the broth. It is the crust of
ground black peppercorns that ties these two elements together superbly, as the heat of the pepper
knifes through the fat tuna and pungent broth. The leeks act as a cleansing element, too,
a refreshing natural foil. Then, as a playful addition, we have the gnocchi, little melt-away
dumplings that contribute the perfect amount of substance.*

Serves 4

*1 12-ounce tuna loin, cut lengthwise
into 2 pieces*
1 tablespoon olive oil
*2 teaspoons coarsely ground black
peppercorns*
½ tablespoon grapeseed oil
½ tablespoon butter
Salt and pepper
½ cup julienned leeks
*1 cup Red Wine-Wild Mushroom-Foie Gras
Broth (recipe follows)*
Potato Gnocchi (recipe follows)

METHOD Rub the tuna with the olive oil
and coat it with the ground peppercorns.
Heat the grapeseed oil and butter in a
medium sauté pan over medium-high heat
and sauté the tuna on all sides for 3 to 5
minutes total. The tuna should still be
quite raw. Poach the leeks in boiling, salted
water until soft, about 5 minutes. Remove
and season with salt and pepper.

ASSEMBLY Cut the tuna into 16 even slices,
arrange 4 slices in each bowl, and place a
little mound of poached leeks in the center.
Spoon ¼ cup of Red Wine-Wild Mushroom-Foie Gras Broth into each bowl and
strew a dozen or so warm gnocchi around
the tuna.

Potato Gnocchi

*2 medium potatoes (about 1 pound),
cooked, peeled, and riced*
1 egg yolk
¼ to 1 cup flour
Salt

METHOD Work the yolk into the potato
with a wooden spoon and knead in enough
flour so that the dough is not sticky. Season
with salt. Divide the mixture into 4 parts.
Roll each part into a long cigar shape about
½-inch in diameter. Cut into ½-inch pieces
and delicately pinch the pieces in the middle. Hold on a lightly floured pan in the
refrigerator until ready to cook. Shortly
before serving, poach 4 dozen gnocchi in
boiling salted water until they float, about
4 to 5 minutes. Remove with a slotted
spoon. (To add an interesting textural element to the dish, sauté the gnocchi in a little butter at this point.)

Put the extra gnocchi on a sheet pan lined
with parchment and freeze; store in plastic
bags in the freezer. To cook, do not defrost.
Just drop the frozen gnocchi into boiling
water and add a little extra cooking time.

Red Wine-Wild Mushroom-Foie Gras Broth

1 cup Wild Mushroom Stock (see Appendix)
¼ cup Red Wine Reduction (see Appendix)
*3 tablespoons Foie Gras Butter
(see Appendix)*
Salt and pepper

METHOD Combine the Wild Mushroom
Stock and Red Wine Reduction in a small
saucepan and bring to a boil. Whisk in the
Foie Gras Butter and season with salt and
pepper. Serve warm.

Wine Notes

This hearty preparation's earthy, rich aromas and flavors create the right atmo-
sphere for a full-bodied red wine. The
intense pepper presents a textural complexity best countered by a ripe wine such
as a Tuscan red. The Red Wine Reduction
that forms the base of the broth reinforces
the need for some balancing acidity in the
wine, yet the delicacy of the tuna begs for a
softer wine, like Merlot. Castello di Ama
makes single-vineyard Chiantis in many
styles, but the La Casuccia, with 15 percent
Merlot, is the most opulent, and makes the
best companion on the table with this dish.

Seared Raw Tuna with Curried Carrot Broth, Collard Greens, and Baby Carrots

*The combination of rare tuna with a curry-flavored carrot broth turns out
to be an unexpectedly happy merger. The broth has a potency, yet at the same time
an ethereal quality that allows the dish to seem hearty yet still quite light.
The delicate acidity in the braised collard greens nicely offsets the sweetness of the carrot broth,
and the broth itself is beautifully echoed by the caramelized baby carrots.*

Serves 4

3 tablespoons chopped bacon

*2 cups cleaned, coarsely chopped
collard greens*

3 tablespoons rice vinegar

1 12-ounce tuna loin

1 tablespoon olive oil

1 teaspoon ground black pepper

½ teaspoon curry powder

1½ teaspoons grapeseed oil

6 tablespoons unsalted butter

1 onion, coarsely sliced

20 to 24 baby carrots, peeled

Salt and pepper

Curried Carrot Broth (recipe follows)

METHOD Render the bacon fat in a small saucepan; remove the bacon while still soft and reserve. Add the collard greens and rice vinegar to the saucepan, cover and braise over low heat for 10 to 12 minutes, until well cooked. If you have tough collard greens and need a longer cooking time, you may need to add a little water to the pan. In the meantime, rub the tuna loin with the olive oil, ground black pepper, and curry powder. Heat the grapeseed oil and 1 tablespoon of butter in a large sauté pan over medium-high heat, and sauté the tuna on all sides for 3 to 4 minutes total. Remove from the pan to a warm place and season with a little salt. Return the bacon to the pan with the collard greens and season with salt and pepper. In a separate pan, melt 3 tablespoons of butter over low heat, and stew the onions until they are very soft and translucent. Season with salt and pepper.

Sauté the tiny carrots in the remaining 2 tablespoons of butter over medium heat for 4 to 5 minutes or until they just begin to caramelize. Season with salt and pepper.

ASSEMBLY Spoon the onions into the center of each bowl. Distribute the collard greens on top of the onions. Slice the tuna loin into 20 or so thin pieces and fan them evenly across the collard greens. Strew the carrots around the greens and pour about ¼ cup of the Curried Carrot Broth into each bowl.

Curried Carrot Broth

2 tablespoons minced onion

1 tablespoon minced apple

2 teaspoons curry powder

2 tablespoons plus ½ cup unsalted butter

2 cups Carrot Juice (see Appendix)

Salt and pepper

METHOD Stew the onion, apple, and curry powder in 2 tablespoons of butter for 10 minutes or so. Cool and blend in a small food processor for about 30 seconds. Add the remaining ½ cup of butter and process another 30 seconds or so. Pass this through a fine strainer.

Bring the Carrot Juice to a simmer. Whisk in 4 tablespoons of the flavored butter and season with salt and pepper. It must be served immediately.

Wine Notes

The seductive, sweet aromas and flavors of the curry, carrot, and apple demand an aromatic, lighter-bodied wine with an emphasis on fruit rather than oak. White Rhône varieties such as Marsanne would be an appropriate match. New World versions by Preston and Qupé supply the richness needed to complement the tuna and its peppery crust and enough tartness to balance the bacon's smokiness. For a more intense wine, choose a Roussanne-based wine like Bonny Doon's exotic *Le Sophiste* or the rare Alban Vineyards Roussanne.

RABBIT

—◆◆◆—

Rabbit is my answer to serving chicken at the restaurant; it is my way of offering a delicate, light meat. I prefer it to chicken because I think it has a more interesting flavor. Rabbit can be prepared any number of ways. I braise the leg or make it into a confit, pan-sear or grill the loins — I even get playful and serve a rack of rabbit like a rack of lamb. For most of the loin preparations, it is best to leave the meat just a bit underdone since rabbit is very lean and can easily become overcooked and dry. Depending on the preparation, rabbit can be offered as a very elegant light course before a more full-bodied beef, lamb, or squab dish, or it can be served as an entrée on its own, perfect for a summer dinner.

Stores that sell natural meats should carry fresh rabbit or be able to order it for you. A good butcher should be able to obtain it as well, though it may take a few days notice. As a last resort there is always mail order through a specialty purveyor (see source list). All of the recipes that follow could also be made with pheasant, poussin, or even chicken; the flavor combinations would not be terribly altered.

Rabbit Rillette in Crispy Phyllo with Oranges, Olives, and Rabbit Stock Reduction

The rabbit meat in this preparation is so sweet and tender, it absolutely melts away. The crispy phyllo casing adds a wonderful aspect of elegance to the dish, and also serves as a crunchy foil to the soft, sweet meat. The oranges, olives, and bits of roasted bell pepper give this dish a Mediterranean touch that makes it ideally suited for warmer weather. Finally, the spicy, salty olives lend a bit of bite. In all, it is a superb combination of flavors.

Serves 4

6 cured rabbit legs (recipe follows)

6 to 8 cups duck fat

Salt and pepper

1½ tablespoons finely chopped green bell pepper

1½ tablespoons finely chopped red bell pepper

3 teaspoons olive oil

4 cloves garlic, minced

40 large spinach leaves, cleaned and stemmed

12 phyllo leaves, cut into 9 x 13-inch rectangles

4 to 6 tablespoons melted butter

2 teaspoons chopped tarragon

2 teaspoons chopped sage

8 slices peeled Valencia orange

1½ tablespoons Spanish green olives, chopped

1½ tablespoons Ligurian black olives, chopped

½ Roasted Red Bell Pepper, cut into 24 diamond-shaped pieces (see Appendix)

⅔ cup Rabbit Stock Reduction (see Appendix)

1 tablespoon assorted chopped or snipped herbs (e.g., tarragon, rosemary, chervil, basil, etc.)

METHOD Braise the cured rabbit legs in enough duck fat to cover for 3 to 4 hours. Drain the rabbit legs, discarding the fat and liquid. Remove the bones and shred the meat with a fork. Season to taste with salt and pepper. (This may be done a day ahead, wrapped in plastic, and refrigerated.)

In a medium pan, sauté the chopped green and red bell peppers lightly in 2 teaspoons of olive oil. In a separate pan, lightly sauté the garlic in 1 teaspoon of olive oil. Working it with a fork, warm the rillette mixture slowly over a bain-marie until just room temperature. Fold the sautéed bell peppers and garlic into the rillette. Season with salt and pepper, if necessary. Blanch the spinach leaves in boiling water, immediately shock them in ice water, and blot them dry.

Lay 4 phyllo sheets out on a flat, dry surface. Brush carefully with melted butter (a paint brush works well), lightly covering the whole surface. Sprinkle a little tarragon and sage on each sheet of phyllo, and place another piece of phyllo on top. Brush with butter, sprinkle with herbs, and top with another sheet of phyllo. Brush lightly with butter. Divide the blanched spinach leaves and lay them out in a rectangle along the 9-inch side on each stack of phyllo. They will cover about ⅓ of the phyllo sheet. Spread a thin layer of the rabbit rillette (about ½ to ¾ cup) on the spinach and, beginning with the spinach end, roll up each stack of phyllo like a cigar. Place on a nonstick sheet pan or on parchment. Brush with a little melted butter. Bake at 475 degrees for 10 minutes or so until golden and crispy. Warm the slices of orange briefly in a 350-degree oven.

ASSEMBLY Place 2 slices of orange on the center of each plate. Strew the green and black olives and a few pieces of roasted bell pepper around each plate. Cut each phyllo roll on the diagonal into 3 or 4 pieces and place them on the oranges. Drizzle the Rabbit Stock Reduction around each plate and strew with herbs.

Cured Rabbit

2 tablespoons kosher salt

2 tablespoons sugar

6 bay leaves, crumbled

2 thyme sprigs

6 cloves garlic, chopped

6 strands julienned ginger

6 rabbit legs

METHOD Combine the first six ingredients together and rub thoroughly into the meat. Refrigerate for 48 hours, then thoroughly rinse off the mixture.

Wine Notes

The phyllo, citrus, and olive elements of this preparation are Mediterranean influences that might suggest a ripe, yet soft, red wine from the region, like a lush Minervois, or Mas de Gourgonnier Rouge. Yet the high acidity of the orange provides its own counterpoint to the dish's rich, savory olive and herb flavors, so a white wine of greater tartness could also work well. A Zind-Humbrecht Riesling from a lower yield vintage, such as 1991, has just the raciness to complement the rich rabbit and olive flavors, while echoing the orange hint in its own right. If you wish to accentuate these flavors even more, try an intense Sauvignon Blanc from a New Zealand producer. The 1992 Cloudy Bay is a revelation, with citrus and herbal hints that seem to fuse all the flavors beautifully.

Seared Rabbit Loin with Braised Legumes and Cumin-Infused Sweet Corn Broth

<hr>

Rabbit, cumin, and beans seem to work together perfectly, and with the addition of a little corn, you have an ideal early fall preparation. This dish is light and delicate, yet richly satisfying due to the beans. The broth adds an exotic accent and the rabbit provides a depth of flavor.

Serves 4

4 rabbit loins

1½ teaspoons cracked black pepper

2½ tablespoons olive oil

2 teaspoons minced garlic

3 bay leaves, crumbled

Salt and pepper

1½ cups Braised Legumes (recipe follows)

2 tomatillos, blanched and diced

¼ cup sweet corn kernels (about 1 ear)

6 ears baby corn, blanched and cut into thin slices

⅓ cup diced Roasted Red Bell Pepper (see Appendix)

⅔ cup Sweet Corn Broth (see Appendix)

2 tablespoons Compound Cumin Butter (recipe follows)

Chervil sprigs

METHOD Marinate the rabbit loins in the refrigerator overnight in the black pepper, 1½ tablespoons olive oil, garlic, and bay leaf. Heat the remaining tablespoon of olive oil in a medium nonstick sauté pan over medium-high heat. Season the rabbit loins with salt, and carefully place them in the pan. Cook on all sides until golden brown and just past medium-rare in the center, about 3 to 4 minutes. Remove from the pan and allow to rest for 2 to 3 minutes in a warm spot. In the meantime, toss the legumes, tomatillos, sweet corn, baby corn, and bell pepper in the pan. Season with salt and pepper and cook until thoroughly heated. Heat the Sweet Corn Broth, stir in the Compound Cumin Butter, and season with salt and pepper.

ASSEMBLY Spoon the vegetables onto 4 plates. Cut each rabbit loin into 5 or 6 pieces and arrange them on the vegetables. Spoon hot broth over all, and garnish with chervil.

Braised Legumes

1 carrot, cleaned and chopped

1 celery stalk, cleaned and chopped

1 small onion, peeled and chopped

1 bay leaf, broken into pieces

1 clove garlic, chopped

About ½ cup butter

1 cup assorted legumes (e.g., black-eyed peas, flageolets, black beans, limas, and scarlet runners)

METHOD Combine the carrot, celery, onion, bay leaf, garlic and 2 tablespoons of butter in a medium sauté pan. Cook over low heat until thoroughly caramelized. Place each type of legume in a different saucepan, and divide the vegetable mixture equally among the saucepans. Add to each pan 2 tablespoons of butter and enough water to cover the legumes. Cook over very low heat until the beans are tender (cooking times will vary depending on the legumes used.)

Compound Cumin Butter

1 teaspoon cumin

1 tablespoon water

2 tablespoons softened unsalted butter

METHOD Warm the cumin and water and stir to make a paste. Mix the cumin paste into the butter.

Wine Notes

Spicy cumin takes the aromatic center of this dish, and becomes the major palate flavor to contend with as well. Because hot spices can be exaggerated by higher alcohol wines, the best way to minimize this effect is to choose a low-alcohol wine such as Mosel Kabinett or Spätlese Halbtrocken, for example, the Zeltinger Sonnenuhr Riesling Spätlese Halbtrocken 1992 from Fruhmesse-Stiftung. These light wines also bear appropriate fruit and sweetness levels to match up to the sweet corn and bell pepper. The fairly high acidity enlivens the soft texture of the legumes, and the rabbit meat itself carries all these flavors without being drowned out, as it might be with a more powerful wine.

Braised Rabbit Leg with Sweet Potatoes, Celery Root, and Thyme-Infused Rabbit Stock Reduction

*This hearty dish offers a fullness of flavor, and yet it is not overly rich. The sweet potatoes
and the celery root contribute a subtle earthiness that complements the delicate flavor and texture of
the rabbit, and the clean, light reduction sauce ties all of the elements together beautifully.
This is an excellent dish to serve when the weather turns chilly.*

Serves 4

4 rabbit legs

1 tablespoon Dijon mustard

2 tablespoons olive oil

4 sage leaves, coarsely chopped

4 cloves garlic, peeled and sliced

4 bay leaves, crumbled

*2 teaspoons black peppercorns,
lightly crushed*

½ cup peeled and chopped onion

½ cup peeled and chopped carrot

½ cup peeled and chopped celery

4 cloves garlic, peeled and chopped

4 tablespoons rendered bacon fat

3 to 4 cups Chicken Stock (see Appendix)

3 thyme sprigs

2 bay leaves

5 parsley sprigs

1 medium tomato, concassée

½ cup julienned celery root

2 cups milk

*1 medium sweet potato, peeled and cut into
thin discs*

About 5½ tablespoons unsalted butter

Salt and pepper

*½ cup cleaned and sliced shiitake
mushrooms*

METHOD Toss the rabbit legs with the Dijon mustard, olive oil, sage leaves, sliced garlic, bay leaves, and black peppercorns. Marinate overnight in the refrigerator.

In a pan large enough to hold all the legs in one layer, lightly brown the onion, carrot, celery, and chopped garlic in the bacon fat over medium-high heat. Remove the vegetables with a slotted spoon and add the rabbit legs. Brown 2 to 3 minutes on each side. Return the vegetables to the pan, nestling the rabbit legs on top of them, and add the stock, thyme, bay leaves, parsley, and tomato. The legs should be just barely submerged in the liquid. Simmer for 2 hours, adding more stock or water if necessary. Skim away any fat or impurities that may rise to the surface. Remove the legs and strain the vegetables from the liquid. Slowly reduce the liquid down to ⅓ to ½ cup, and set aside.

For the final preparation you will need to keep several pans going at one time. First, put the celery root and milk in a small saucepan and simmer gently until cooked, about 4 to 5 minutes. Heat 1½ tablespoons of butter in a large sauté pan over medium heat and sauté the sweet potatoes in batches (the pieces should not overlap), about 1½ minutes per side, adding more butter as needed. Season with salt and pepper and

remove them to a paper towel. At the same time, in a small pan over medium heat, sauté the shiitake mushrooms in 1½ teaspoons of butter. Season with salt and pepper and remove them to a paper towel. Quickly sauté the rabbit legs in 2 tablespoons of butter and transfer to a 400-degree oven for 8 to 10 minutes to heat thoroughly. Bring the reduced braising liquid to a boil, whisk in 1½ teaspoons of butter, and stir in the parsley. Drain the celery root, season it with salt and pepper, and toss with 1 tablespoon of butter.

ASSEMBLY Arrange the mushrooms around the edges of each plate and place the sweet potatoes in the center. Mound the celery root on top of the sweet potatoes and place a rabbit leg on top. Spoon a few tablespoons of sauce on each serving.

Wine Notes

Lighter red wines come immediately to mind for this slowly cooked *winter* dish and its hearty, sweet flavors of tubers and roots. A sweet-cored Pinot Noir from Santa Barbara County, California, such as the delicate versions by Sanford and Byron, can be a sublime match. This style of Pinot, often chastised for its herbal qualities, will also merge beautifully with the thyme in the reduction sauce.

Rabbit and Braised Turnip Lasagna
with Sweet Pea Sauce

*This dish can really only be made in the early summer, when fresh sweet peas are
in abundance. As the season goes on, they become too starchy and are thus too strong for the light
rabbit and the turnips. Young sweet peas, on the other hand, have a unique,
delicate flavor that puts all the elements of this dish in balance. Once you have tasted the purity
of this sauce, you will never again add cream to a pea sauce.*

Serves 4

2 large turnips, peeled

3 to 4 cups Chicken Stock (see Appendix)

4 rabbit loins

2 tablespoons grapeseed oil

*2 tablespoons Foie Gras Butter
(see Appendix)*

*1 cup Napa cabbage, cut into a
fine chiffonnade*

*½ cup finely julienned small shiitake
mushrooms*

1 teaspoon chopped tarragon

Salt and pepper

2 cups shelled sweet peas

METHOD Braise the turnips in Chicken
Stock to cover until just soft in the middle,
about 25 to 30 minutes. Cool them in the
braising liquid, trim into squares, and slice
very thinly, yielding at least 12 slices per
turnip. Over medium-high heat, sauté the
rabbit loins on all sides in the grapeseed oil.

Turn the heat down to medium and continue cooking for 1½ to 2 minutes, or until
the loins are just barely cooked through. (If
you prefer, the loins can be grilled.)
Remove the meat from the pan and allow
to rest. Using the same pan, melt the Foie
Gras Butter and sauté the shiitake mushrooms and Napa cabbage for 2 to 3 minutes,
shaking the pan or stirring from time to
time. Add the tarragon, season with salt
and pepper, and set aside.

Blanch the peas in boiling salted water for
30 seconds or so, then shock them in ice
water. Setting a few aside for garnish, juice
the peas. For maximum flavor, blanch and
shock the shells, too. They can be blended
with a little water, strained, and added to
the juice from the peas.

ASSEMBLY Slice the rabbit loins thinly on
the bias and make 4 individual lasagne
by layering the loins with the cabbage-
mushroom mixture and the turnip slices.

Place in a 400-degree oven for about 45
seconds to warm thoroughly. Remove to 4
warm bowls. Bring the pea sauce to a delicate boil and warm the reserved peas
briefly. Pour a little sauce into each bowl
and garnish with the peas.

Wine Notes

The turnips in this dish are at once sweet,
earthy, and bitter—the same descriptions
often applied to fine, balanced, young
wines, both red and white. The pea sauce
adds to the sweetness, turning the dish in
the white direction, with a concentrated
Loire Valley Savennières leading the way.
The most sublime example comes from
N. Joly's Clos de la Coulée de Serrant, a
wine of incredible length and texture.
More earthy (and more readily available)
wines come from the Domaine des Bau-
mard, whose *Trie Spéciale* makes a rich
(15 percent alcohol) statement while not
overwhelming the rabbit.

Warm Rabbit Salad with Pommery Pasta, Black Truffle Coulis, and Mâche

~~~~~~

This dish can work either as a salad or as a pasta dish, or possibly even as a main course, depending on the balance of the menu. I especially love the way the sharpness of the mustard in the pasta accentuates the very pungent truffle coulis. The mâche in its delicacy acts as a perfect backdrop to the powerful flavors of both the truffles and the mustard. The rabbit, in this case, becomes the beneficiary of these three perfectly matched flavor components.

Serves 4

4 large rabbit loins
1 tablespoon olive oil
1 tablespoon Pommery mustard
2 teaspoons grapeseed oil
Salt and pepper
4 rabbit kidneys (optional)
80 mâche leaves (or other lettuce)
2 teaspoons coarsely chopped chervil
Pommery Pasta (recipe follows)
Pommery Vinaigrette (recipe follows)
Black Truffle Coulis (recipe follows)

METHOD Rub the rabbit loins with olive oil and mustard and marinate for 2 to 3 hours. If you are serving the kidneys, marinate them along with the loins. Keep refrigerated while making the pasta, the coulis, and the vinaigrette. Heat the grapeseed oil in a medium sauté pan over medium-high heat, and brown the rabbit loins on all sides. Turn the heat down to medium and continue to cook for 2 or 3 minutes or until the loins are just past medium-rare. Season with salt and pepper and remove the loins to a warm spot. If used, sauté the kidneys in the same pan for 3 or 4 minutes until medium. Just before serving, slice the rabbit loins very thinly on the bias and cut the kidneys in half.

ASSEMBLY Toss the pasta with Pommery Vinaigrette and place a mound of pasta in the center of each plate. Place 20 or so mâche leaves around the edges of each plate. Fan 1 sliced loin around each mound of noodles. Drizzle about 1 tablespoon of Black Truffle Coulis onto each salad and sprinkle on the chopped chervil. If using the kidneys, place 2 pieces on each mound of pasta.

Pommery Pasta

3 tablespoons Pommery mustard
1 egg yolk
½ teaspoon salt
1 to 1½ cups semolina flour
2 to 4 tablespoons water

METHOD Whisk together the mustard, yolk, and salt and work it into the flour, adding water a little at a time until the dough comes together. Knead until the dough is smooth, adding small amounts of flour if the dough is sticky. Allow to rest for at least 1 hour. Roll out and cut into the desired width. Shortly before serving, cook in boiling salted water just until al dente, and strain.

Pommery Vinaigrette

1 tablespoon Pommery mustard
1 tablespoon lemon juice

3 tablespoons olive oil
Salt and pepper

METHOD Whisk together the mustard, lemon juice, and olive oil, and season to taste with salt and pepper.

Black Truffle Coulis

1 black truffle, about the size of a walnut
1 to 2 tablespoons grapeseed oil
2 tablespoons truffle oil
2 teaspoons water
1 teaspoon lemon juice
Salt and pepper to taste

METHOD Slice the truffle and warm it slightly in the grapeseed oil. Purée the truffle with the grapeseed oil, truffle oil, water, and lemon juice. Season with salt and pepper.

Wine Notes

This earthy, heady dish has many friends in wine, but the most striking would be a fine Alsace Gewurztraminer from Domaine Weinbach-Faller, especially from a Grand Cru vineyard. The spiciness of the wine, embellished by floral and litchi aromas, is incredibly stimulating, as are the Pommery mustard tang and the perfume of truffles in the rabbit salad.

Rack of Rabbit with Braised Cabbage
and Juniper-Infused Rabbit Reduction Sauce

The highly concentrated reduction sauce with its juniper influence makes this the richest rabbit preparation that I serve. It is suitable as a main course, to be served in place of lamb or venison. Boning a rabbit to imitate racks of lamb is certainly time-consuming, but the visual result is quite stunning, making this treatment appropriate for special occasions —perhaps a New Year's Eve dinner. In order to bone out the racks, you must start with whole rabbits. The legs can be saved for another meal.

Serves 4

2 whole rabbits

4 teaspoons grapeseed oil

1 teaspoon juniper berries, roasted in a small skillet and ground

½ teaspoon black peppercorns, roasted and ground

1 cup Savoy cabbage, cut into a fine chiffonade

1 tablespoon butter

1½ teaspoons champagne vinegar or cider vinegar

2 tablespoons Chicken Stock (see Appendix)

2 tablespoons julienned McIntosh apple

2 tablespoons bacon, finely diced and sautéed until crisp

1 teaspoon sage, cut into a fine chiffonade

Salt and pepper

1 tablespoon each carrot, celery, and red bell pepper, cut into a fine brunoise

Juniper-Infused Rabbit Reduction (recipe follows)

METHOD To prepare the racks, cut each rabbit in half widthwise just below the last rib bone. Cut the rib portion in half along the backbone. Scrape the bones clean down to the loin, being very careful not to damage the soft bones. Toss the rabbit racks in 2 teaspoons of grapeseed oil, ½ teaspoon ground juniper berries, and ground black pepper, and marinate for 6 to 8 hours.

Season the racks with a little salt and pepper and sauté them in an ovenproof pan in 1 teaspoon of grapeseed oil over high heat until thoroughly browned on all sides, about 1 to 2 minutes. Place the pan in a 500-degree oven for 2 to 3 minutes or until the meat is just shy of medium in the center. Remove the racks from the pan and keep warm. Toss the cabbage in the pan with the butter. When the butter melts and the cabbage just begins to stew, deglaze with the vinegar. Add the stock and slowly braise about 4 to 5 minutes. Add the apple, bacon, remaining juniper, and sage, and stew for 30 seconds or so. Season with salt and pepper. Sauté the vegetable *brunoise* in the remaining grapeseed oil until warmed through.

ASSEMBLY Spoon the cabbage onto 4 warm plates and strew some of the vegetable *brunoise* about the edges of the plates. Cut the racks into chops and arrange them on the plates with the meat resting against the cabbage. Drizzle a little warmed reduction sauce onto each plate.

Juniper-Infused Rabbit Reduction

2 pounds rabbit bones

Grapeseed oil

20 juniper berries

1 leek, chopped

3 cloves garlic

3 cups red wine

1 quart Chicken Stock (see Appendix)

Sage sprigs

METHOD Chop up the rabbit bones and sauté them in a *rondeau* with a little grapeseed oil. Toss in the juniper berries, leek, and garlic, and sauté for several minutes. Deglaze with the red wine and the Chicken Stock. Reduce slowly for 10 minutes and strain through a fine strainer. Continue to reduce to about ⅔ cup. Steep a little sage in the sauce for 30 seconds or so, and strain again.

Wine Notes

While the bacon and the intense sauce in this preparation seem to point to a red wine selection, the tiny rabbit *chops* are so elegant, they could easily be overwhelmed by such a choice. Considering the dish's placement as a main course, a lighter style of Burgundy makes sense, like the delicate Cortons of Prince de Mérode, but an argument can be made for a rich Alsace Riesling as well. The juniper-infused stock can be well met by a Domaine Weinbach Grand Cru from Schlossberg or a Zind-Humbrecht Rangen de Thann, while not overwhelming the rabbit; and the tartness of these wines can do well with the Savoy cabbage.

SQUAB

Of all the types of game birds that can grace the table, squab is certainly my favorite. In fact, it is probably my favorite meat altogether. I love it because it is rich and succulent, and has a most complex and interesting flavor, yet it is also quite lean. It does not, however, dry out as easily as other lean birds such as pheasant or poussin. In addition, it lends itself well to a variety of preparations: it can be grilled, sautéed, braised, or smoked with excellent results. You can even serve it raw in the form of a carpaccio. Usually I like a bit of sweetness with my pigeon—perhaps a little roasted garlic, preserved ginger, dried fruits, or very old balsamic vinegar. The key is to keep the composition subtle so that the squab is never overpowered.

I use only fresh, naturally raised birds from California, but you can probably find a source close to you. Many specialty markets routinely carry it, or can easily order it for you. I even know a health food store in Chicago that carries it on a regular basis. If you are unable to find squab, you can substitute duck breast in the following recipes (with the exception of the carpaccio), but you would have to modify the cooking process to take into account the fattiness of that bird. Pheasant and chicken breast could also be used.

Because of the richness of the meat, I typically make my squab preparations work with red wines. If you substitute lighter-meated birds such as pheasant or chicken, you should alter the wine accompaniment accordingly.

Squab Breast with Garlic-Herb Tuiles, Salsify, and Papaya

~~~~~~

Salsify has a subtle and complex flavor that I have really grown to appreciate. At times it exhibits characteristics of artichoke or even asparagus—especially when it is paired with a little mild fruit. In this dish, I have combined a purée of salsify with crispy garlic tuiles, perfectly ripe papaya, and succulent squab breast. This preparation could work either as an appetizer or a main course.

Serves 4

2 teaspoons grapeseed oil

2 squab breasts, boned and halved

Salt and pepper

1 salsify root

About 1 cup milk

1 tablespoon butter

1 teaspoon snipped chives

Salsify Purée (recipe follows)

4 Garlic-Herb Tuiles (recipe follows)

½ cup ripe papaya, cut into a brunoise

*½ cup Squab Stock Reduction
(see Appendix)*

METHOD Heat the grapeseed oil in a medium pan over medium-high heat. Place the squab breasts in the pan skin side down and cook for 1½ to 2 minutes, then turn and cook for 30 to 40 seconds more. Remove from the pan, season with salt and pepper, and allow to rest for 2 or 3 minutes in a warm spot.

Peel and julienne the salsify. Immediately put it in a container with enough milk to cover. To cook, drain the salsify and pat dry; melt the butter in a small sauté pan over medium heat, then sauté for 2 minutes or so. Season with salt and pepper and add the chives.

ASSEMBLY Place 1½ to 2 tablespoons of warm Salsify Purée in the center of each plate. Nestle a Garlic-Herb *Tuile* into each mound of purée. Divide the julienned salsify into each *tuile*. Slice the squab breast into thin pieces and arrange them inside the *tuiles*. Place a couple of mounds of the papaya *brunoise* on each plate and drizzle 2 tablespoons of Squab Stock Reduction around the puréed salsify.

Salsify Purée

2 salsify roots

2 cups milk

*2 to 3 tablespoons Vegetable Stock
(see Appendix)*

Salt and pepper

METHOD Peel the salsify and cut into 1-inch pieces. Place in a small saucepan and add the milk immediately to avoid oxidation of the salsify. Bring to a simmer and cook for 4 to 5 minutes or until soft enough to purée. Drain. Purée in a blender, adding Vegetable Stock a bit at a time to achieve a smooth consistency. If you need to thicken the purée, place it in the top of a double boiler and evaporate some of the water content. This preparation can be done 1 to 2 hours in advance and then heated up in a double boiler when you are ready to serve it.

Garlic-Herb *Tuiles*

3 whole eggs, room temperature

4 egg whites, room temperature

¾ cup Simple Syrup (see Appendix)

*¼ cup meat or Vegetable Stock
(see Appendix)*

*2 cloves Roasted Garlic, puréed
(see Appendix)*

2¼ cups sifted flour

1½ teaspoons minced rosemary

½ pound butter, melted

Salt and pepper

METHOD Whisk together the eggs, egg whites, Simple Syrup, stock, and garlic purée. Work the flour into the mixture, then stir in the rosemary and the melted butter. Season to taste with salt and pepper. On a nonstick sheet pan, thinly spread about 1 tablespoon of the *tuile* mixture into a 5-inch circle. Repeat until the batter is used up. Bake at 375 degrees for 2 to 3 minutes or until lightly browned, then mold into a cup shape by draping the *tuile* over an inverted timbale and pressing it gently into shape. This recipe will make more than you will need for 4 servings, but it is difficult to make a smaller amount. The *tuiles* will remain crisp for a few days if stored in an airtight container.

Wine Notes

The papaya adds a light, sweet touch to this preparation, while the creamy salsify purée is aromatic and well-integrated with the squab meat. In addition, the garlic *tuile* lends a major flavor component that is also somewhat sweet. A very soft Pinot Noir is in order here, and one that expresses riper fruit. Carneros has long been lauded for its fine Pinot Noir fruit qualities, and the recent projects of Robert Mondavi may have produced the finest merging of fruit and winemaking there to date. The Robert Mondavi Carneros Pinot Noir 1991 (produced with natural progressive farming techniques) supports the dish well, while echoing the slight tropical element. Other Carneros producers worth seeking out are Acacia, Saintsbury, and Robert Sinskey.

Squab Salad with Foie Gras Hollandaise, White Truffle Oil, 50-Year-Old Balsamic Vinegar, and Crispy Pig's Feet

Warm salads are hard to beat! Flavors take on added complexity when the salad components are warmed and just barely tossed together. Frisée is a great lettuce for a warm salad because even after it has been slightly wilted, it retains a nice texture. The multiple flavors in this dish add an amazing depth. Bacon is frequently used in warm salads, but here I have substituted braised Crispy Pig's Feet. This recipe could be doubled and the salad served as a main course, preceded by a soup or a pasta preparation.

Serves 4

1½ cups Chicken Stock (see Appendix)

2 squab breasts, boned, skinned, and halved

2 to 4 teaspoons grapeseed oil

4 squab legs (optional)

Salt and pepper

2 to 3 cups frisée

Foie Gras Hollandaise (recipe follows)

¼ cup Crispy Pig's Feet (see Appendix)

4 teaspoons white truffle oil

4 teaspoons 50-year-old balsamic vinegar

2 teaspoons chopped herbs (e.g., tarragon, thyme, basil, etc.)

METHOD In a small saucepan over medium heat, reduce the Chicken Stock to 2 tablespoons. Heat a medium pan over medium-high heat, sauté the squab breasts in 2 teaspoons of grapeseed oil for 1½ minutes on each side, then roast them in a 400-degree oven for 2 minutes. Remove the breasts, season on both sides with salt and pepper, and allow to rest in a warm place. If you are using the legs, sauté them in 2 teaspoons of grapeseed oil for 2 to 3 minutes, turning every 30 seconds. Remove the legs from the pan, season, and allow to rest in a warm place.

Add the frisée to the pan, still over medium heat, and toss quickly for 30 seconds. Season lightly and remove.

ASSEMBLY Spoon about 2 tablespoons of Foie Gras Hollandaise into the center of each plate and arrange the frisée on top of it. Cut each squab breast into 6 or 7 slices, and arrange them around the frisée. If you are serving the squab legs, place one atop each mound of lettuce. Strew the pig's feet around the plates. Drizzle the reduced Chicken Stock, white truffle oil, and 50-year-old balsamic vinegar on and around the greens. Sprinkle a few herbs on top and serve.

Foie Gras Hollandaise

This recipe makes more than is necessary for 4 servings, but it is difficult to make a smaller amount.

2 egg yolks

2 teaspoons rice vinegar

⅓ pound Foie Gras Butter (see Appendix)

1 tablespoon white truffle oil

Salt and pepper

METHOD Whisk the yolks and vinegar in a bowl over boiling water until aerated. Whisk in the butter bit by bit. Whisk in the white truffle oil and season to taste with salt and pepper.

Wine Notes

The intense, diverse aromas of the dish make Syrah seem enticing, even a powerful example like Côte Rôtie, but the delicacy of the salad requires a far less intense wine. Columbia Woodburne Cuvée Pinot Noir 1989 is a rare match for this preparation, with its very light body and ethereal Pinot expression. Other suitable light Pinots include the Domaine Bertheau Chambolle-Musigny 1988 and the Handley Anderson Valley.

Squab Breast with Crispy Curry Noodles and Spiced Consommé

~~~~~~

This dish would make an ideal transition course between raw or marinated seafood and a heartier entrée, such as lamb or venison. In it, the heady, full-flavored squab meat is perfectly complemented by an exotically spiced consommé, and the crispy noodles add a nice textural element. Finally, the addition of the Chiogga beets gives the dish a sweet edge that suits the meat and the spices nicely.

Serves 4

2 squab breasts, halved

2 teaspoons hazelnut oil

1 teaspoon curry powder

2 tablespoons apple juice

1 leek, cleaned

1 to 1½ cups Squab or Chicken Consommé (see Appendix)

2 tablespoons mixed allspice, clove, cinnamon, cumin, crushed red pepper flakes, and ginger, tied in a spice bag

Salt and pepper

1 tablespoon grapeseed oil

Crispy Curry Noodles (recipe follows)

Squab Liver Mousse (see Appendix)

4 Chiogga beets, blanched, peeled, and cut into small pieces

METHOD Bone the squab breasts, leaving the skin on. Warm the hazelnut oil and curry briefly to marry the flavors and bring out the oils in the curry, and thus the fullest flavor. Mix the *curry oil* with the apple juice, and thoroughly massage this into the squab breasts on all sides. Refrigerate for 6 to 8 hours before assembling the dish.

Poach the leek in boiling, salted water for several minutes until it is just cooked. Remove and slice into disks. Bring the con-sommé to a boil. Drop the spice bag into it and allow to steep for 45 seconds to 1 minute. Remove the spice bag and adjust the seasoning with salt and pepper.

Heat the grapeseed oil in a medium sauté pan. Sauté the squab breasts skin side down for 1½ to 2 minutes, then turn and sauté for another 30 to 45 seconds. Remove from the pan, season, and allow to rest for 2 to 3 minutes in a warm spot.

ASSEMBLY Place a few slices of leek in the center of each bowl. Place a galette of Crispy Curry Noodles on top of the leeks, followed by a little Squab Liver Mousse. Thinly slice the squab breasts and fan the meat on top of the mousse. Add a few warm beet pieces to each bowl, and pour in ¼ to ⅓ cup of consommé.

Crispy Curry Noodles

1 tablespoon curry powder

1 egg

1 cup semolina flour

2 teaspoons hazelnut oil

Salt and pepper

2 teaspoons butter

METHOD Whisk together the curry powder and egg. Work in the flour a little at a time until the dough comes together. Knead until the dough is smooth, adding small amounts of flour if the dough is sticky. Allow to rest for 1 hour. Roll out and cut into desired width.

Cook the noodles in boiling, salted water until just al dente. Drain and immediately plunge into ice water until completely cooled. Drain again, toss with the hazelnut oil, and season with a little salt and pepper. Line a roasting pan or cookie sheet with plastic wrap and lay the noodles in a flat square ¾ inch high. Cover with plastic wrap and place another roasting pan on top. Weight with a brick or a similarly heavy object and refrigerate for at least 6 to 8 hours. Then cut the noodles into 4 triangles or other desired shape.

Just before serving, heat the butter over medium heat in a nonstick pan and sauté the noodles on both sides until golden and crispy.

Wine Notes

This rendition of squab presents delicacy and zing at the same time, but the overall effect is understated. A relatively mature Burgundy will enhance the cinnamon, clove, and allspice with its advanced oakiness. A delicate Premier Cru Nuits St.-Georges from Domaine Boillot is especially apt. Another interestingly spicy wine is the Pernand-Vergelesses by the Domaine Chandon de Briailles.

Squab Breast Carpaccio with Tomato Chutney Juice and Spaghetti Squash Salad

~~~~~~

This is a fantastic way to appreciate the delicate, rich flavor of squab.
The fact that squab is considered a red meat and does not have the same characteristics as
domestic poultry allows for a preparation such as this one. The barely crisp vegetables
act as a perfect foil to the meat. The nicely acidic juice from the chutney, applied at the last moment,
tenderizes the squab just enough to allow it to disappear in your mouth.

Serves 4

2 squab breasts, boned, skinned, and halved

2 tablespoons plus 2 teaspoons hazelnut oil

Thyme sprigs

2 cloves garlic, peeled and sliced

1 teaspoon minced ginger

1 tablespoon black peppercorns

¼ cup chutney juice, strained from tomato or mango chutney

¼ cup currants

½ cup cooked spaghetti squash

1 small carrot, cut into bâtonnets *and blanched*

Salt and pepper

Thyme petals

METHOD Marinate the squab breasts overnight in 2 tablespoons of hazelnut oil, thyme, sliced garlic, minced ginger, and the black peppercorns. Two to 3 hours before serving, rub the marinade off the squab breasts, wrap them individually in plastic, and freeze.

To obtain the chutney juice, pour some chutney into a very fine mesh strainer and press it lightly with a ladle to render the desired amount. Warm the chutney juice, add the currants, and let macerate off heat for 1 hour. Just before serving, cut each squab breast into 8 or 9 paper-thin slices (an electric slicer works best for this). Toss the spaghetti squash and carrots with the remaining hazelnut oil and season lightly with salt and pepper.

ASSEMBLY Arrange the sliced squab on 4 slightly chilled plates. Spoon about 2 tablespoons each of chutney juice and currants onto each serving, and sprinkle with a little salt and pepper. Distribute the squash and carrots on the plates, and sprinkle a few thyme petals onto the meat.

Wine Notes

Thyme and pepper contribute zestiness to this lively dish, and the crunchy vegetables provide a textural counterpoint to the rich, marinated meat. If it is an early course, wine choices might include a crisp herbal Sancerre such as *Les Culs de Beaujeu* from Cotat or even Cotat's Rosé. Both wines are aggressive enough for the spicy elements and rich enough for the meat, while refreshing the palate with each sip. If a red is desired, another Loire wine could be useful: the Chinon from a good producer like Charles Joguet or Couly-Dutheuil, whose Cabernet Franc is richly extracted yet *green* enough to refresh.

LAMB

When I think of lamb, I think of Provence, and a shoulder of lamb rubbed with garlic and rosemary, grilled slowly over a fire until the meat just melts off the bone. That and a chewy, rich red wine add up to a perfect early spring evening. Or, when I want to give myself the ultimate treat, I prepare a rack of lamb with roasted Ruby Crescent potatoes and a sauce simply made from the juices of the meat, and I open a great Bordeaux. Even though lamb can stand up to strong flavors, I sometimes serve it with delicate accompaniments in order to really show off its elegant character. As with squab, I like to pair it with a touch of sweetness for contrast — some chutney, or a bit of sweet corn or roasted garlic, perhaps. It also works very well with such exotic spices as cumin or coriander, and even with accents that are not traditional with lamb, like tamari sauce or sesame oil.

I buy whole baby lambs from farms in Virginia and Wisconsin. The lambs are grass-fed and naturally raised, and their flavor is remarkable. Occasionally I work with lamb from New Mexico, which has an even fuller, gamier flavor.

Peppered Lamb Loin with Polenta, Ratatouille, and Bell Pepper-Infused Lamb Stock Reduction

~~~~~~

Off and on, I have served this dish in one form or another since the restaurant first opened, and it has always been hugely successful. In this version, the Ratatouille and crispy polenta make the perfect backdrop for the succulent, peppery lamb. Though it is not absolutely necessary, I like to serve it with a little Rouille for an added tang.

Serves 4

1 12-to-16-ounce trimmed lamb loin

6 or 7 tablespoons olive oil

4 tablespoons cracked black pepper

4 cloves garlic, peeled and sliced

½ teaspoon cumin

½ bunch thyme sprigs

1½ cups hot cooked polenta

5 to 6 tablespoons butter

*1 teaspoon chopped herbs
(e.g., rosemary, thyme, basil, etc.)*

*2 tablespoons diced Roasted Red Bell Pepper
(see Appendix)*

4 shallots, peeled and chopped

*1 bunch spinach (about 8 cups), stemmed
and cleaned*

Salt and pepper

Ratatouille (recipe follows)

*Bell Pepper-Infused Lamb Stock Reduction
(recipe follows)*

Rouille (recipe follows)

*3 tablespoons julienned Roasted Red Bell
Pepper (see Appendix)*

Thyme for garnish

METHOD Toss the lamb loin with 4 tablespoons of olive oil, cracked pepper, garlic, cumin, and thyme, and marinate overnight. Mix soft, just-cooked polenta with 1 tablespoon of butter, herbs, and diced bell pepper. Smooth the mixture out on a flat surface about ⅓ inch thick, cover with plastic wrap, and cool for several hours. Sauté the shallots in 1 tablespoon of butter until soft; add the spinach and continue cooking for a couple of minutes until the spinach is just wilted. Season with salt and pepper. Heat 2 tablespoons of olive oil over medium-high heat, sear the lamb on all sides for 2 to 3 minutes, then finish in a 450-degree

oven for 8 to 10 minutes. Remove from oven and allow to rest for 3 to 5 minutes. Meanwhile, cut out 4 3½-inch circles of polenta (or desired shape), and sauté them in butter or olive oil until crispy.

ASSEMBLY Place a small mound of Ratatouille in the center of each plate. Place a little sautéed spinach on each mound and top with a crispy disk of polenta. Top the polenta with about 2 tablespoons of Ratatouille. Slice the lamb loin and fan out the slices on top of the polenta. Place a small amount of Rouille in the center of the lamb. Drizzle a small amount of sauce on each plate, and garnish with the julienned red pepper and fresh thyme leaves. For a precise presentation, layer the Ratatouille, spinach, and polenta inside a 3½-inch cutter.

Ratatouille

4 cloves garlic, chopped

½ cup diced onion

2 to 3 tablespoons olive oil

3 medium tomatoes, concassée

1 medium red bell pepper

1 small fennel bulb

½ medium eggplant

2 small zucchini

Salt and pepper

METHOD Sweat the garlic and onion in 1 tablespoon of olive oil. Add the tomatoes and cook for 5 minutes. Purée and strain, discarding the solids. Cut the pepper, fennel, eggplant, and zucchini into a very fine julienne and sauté them one by one in a little olive oil until they are just cooked. Combine all the cooked vegetables with the tomato sauce, season with salt and pepper, and set aside. Reheat just before serving.

Bell Pepper-Infused Lamb Stock Reduction

1 red bell pepper, seeded and chopped

2 cups Lamb Stock (see Appendix)

METHOD Place the bell pepper in a saucepan with the stock. Slowly reduce down to ⅓ cup and strain. Reheat before serving.

Rouille

Tiny pinch of saffron threads

1 egg yolk

2 cloves Roasted Garlic (see Appendix)

*2 to 3 tablespoons Roasted Red Bell Pepper,
chopped (see Appendix)*

1½ teaspoons Dijon mustard

3 tablespoons olive oil

½ to ⅔ cup grapeseed oil

Salt and white pepper

METHOD Steep the saffron in 2 teaspoons warm water for 2 or 3 minutes. In a food processor, blend the yolk, garlic, bell pepper, mustard, and saffron for 30 seconds or so. With the processor running, slowly drizzle in the olive oil, then the grapeseed oil, until you achieve a desired consistency (like mayonnaise). Season with salt and white pepper. Refrigerate until used.

Wine Notes

The warm Provençal flavors of the Ratatouille and the soft, sweet element of the polenta seem perfect for a ripe, red Mediterranean wine. Rich lamb loin with pepper begs for one from southern France. A hearty southern Rhône can work well, but the ideal flavors come from a Mourvèdre-based wine. Bandol, with its dense, meaty earthiness, can shine; and in particular, the unique wines of Domaine Tempier will make this dish sing.

Truffled Lamb Tartare with Chanterelle Mushroom Salad, Radish Salad, Mushroom Juice, and Watercress Oil

This is a very simple preparation, ideally suited for summertime. The Watercress Oil balances the rich, earthy Mushroom Juice, and at the same time graces the whole with a delicate spiciness. A little julienned radish on the plate provides the perfect, sharp cleansing effect.

Serves 4

2 trimmed lamb tenderloins, about 6 ounces in all

½ tablespoon white truffle oil

2 teaspoons chopped black truffle

1 teaspoon chopped herbs (e.g., rosemary, thyme, basil, etc.)

½ small shallot, peeled and chopped

Salt and pepper

Chanterelle Mushroom Salad (recipe follows)

Radish Salad (recipe follows)

Watercress Oil (recipe follows)

Mushroom Juice (recipe follows)

METHOD Chop the lamb into a very fine dice. Toss the meat with the white truffle oil. Add the black truffle, herbs, and shallots, season to taste with salt and pepper, and refrigerate until ready to serve. Just before serving, using two spoons to help shape them, make 16 quenelles of the tartare.

ASSEMBLY Place 4 quenelles on each plate. Place a little of the Chanterelle Mushroom Salad in the center of each plate, then 2 little mounds of Radish Salad. Drizzle some Watercress Oil on each plate and some Mushroom Juice over the oil.

Chanterelle Mushroom Salad

2 ounces chanterelle mushrooms (choose the tiniest caps possible)

1 teaspoon olive oil

1 teaspoon white truffle oil

½ teaspoon chopped black truffle

Salt and pepper

METHOD In a small saucepan, sauté the mushrooms in the olive oil over medium-high heat, and then cool. Toss the mushrooms with the truffle oil and the truffle pieces. Season to taste with salt and pepper and refrigerate until ready to use.

Radish Salad

4 medium red radishes, julienned

1 teaspoon lemon juice

Snipped chives

Salt

METHOD Toss the radishes with the lemon juice and chives. Season to taste with a tiny bit of salt and refrigerate until ready to use.

Mushroom Juice

1½ pounds button mushrooms

1 quart water

Salt and pepper

METHOD Place the mushrooms and water in a medium saucepan and bring to a boil. Simmer for 30 minutes and strain, discarding the mushrooms. Slowly reduce the liquid down to ½ cup and season lightly with salt and pepper. Serve warm.

Watercress Oil

2 bunches watercress

1 cup grapeseed oil

1 teaspoon salt

METHOD Blanch the watercress in boiling water for just a brief moment and immediately shock in ice water and drain. In a blender, purée the watercress with the grapeseed oil and salt, and place in the refrigerator for a day or so. Decant. Extra Watercress Oil can be stored for at least a week in the refrigerator and used for salad dressings or in other recipes.

Wine Notes

Truffles and white truffle oil transform this dish into an ethereal taste experience. Because the overall effect is one of delicacy, not power, a dense, powerful Rhône takes us in the wrong direction, and a Syrah, often a friendly companion to lamb, is overwhelming. A young, fruity, red wine makes the most sense. One of the Georges DuBoeuf Cru Beaujolais, such as Chiroubles or Fleurie, lets the herbs and truffles state their theme while supplementing the meat flavors.

Braised Lamb Shank with Saffron Risotto and Garlic-Infused Lamb Stock Reduction

*Given the degustation format at the restaurant, we do not often prepare this sort of dish:
the portions would simply be too big. For certain special wine dinners, however, we have achieved
much success with braised lamb and veal shank preparations, where the dish is part
of a much simpler menu. For the degustation, I might take the braised shank meat off the bone
and serve it folded into a grain or use it as a ravioli filling.*

Serves 4.

4 lamb shanks

Salt and pepper

1½ tablespoons olive oil

1 onion, peeled and coarsely chopped

1 carrot, peeled and coarsely chopped

1 stalk celery, peeled and coarsely chopped

1 head garlic, peeled and coarsely chopped

1 cup red wine

About 2 quarts Lamb Stock (see Appendix)

Saffron Risotto (recipe follows)

*Garlic-Infused Lamb Stock Reduction
(recipe follows)*

METHOD Season the lamb shanks with salt and pepper. Heat the olive oil in a large *rondeau* over medium heat and thoroughly brown the meat on all sides. Remove the shanks. Add the onion, carrot, celery, and garlic to the pot and thoroughly sweat until they are just beginning to turn brown. Deglaze with the red wine. Return the lamb shanks to the pot, add the Lamb Stock, cover, and place in a 250-degree oven for 6 to 8 hours, checking from time to time and adding a little water if necessary. When the shanks seems like they are just about done and the meat is very tender, make the risotto.

ASSEMBLY Spoon some risotto onto each plate and top with a hot lamb shank. Drizzle some Garlic-Infused Lamb Stock Reduction onto each plate and serve.

Saffron Risotto

1 small onion, peeled and chopped

4 cloves garlic

1 tablespoon olive oil

1 tablespoon butter

1 pinch saffron threads

¼ cup Arborio rice

3 to 4 cups simmering water

1 rosemary sprig

Salt and pepper

9 to 12 cloves Roasted Garlic (see Appendix)

METHOD Sweat the onion and garlic in oil and butter until they are just translucent. Add the saffron threads and sauté for a minute or so. Add the rice and sauté for 2 to 3 minutes, thoroughly coating all of the rice with fat. Stirring continuously, add water, little by little, until the rice is about halfway cooked (10 minutes or so.) Add the rosemary and continue adding small amounts of water until the risotto is thoroughly cooked, about 20 to 25 minutes more. The risotto should be just slightly al dente, yet creamy. Remove the rosemary, season to taste with salt and pepper, and stir in the Roasted Garlic.

Garlic-Infused Lamb Stock Reduction

1 onion, peeled and coarsely chopped

1 carrot, peeled and coarsely chopped

2 stalks celery, peeled and coarsely chopped

3 heads garlic, peeled and coarsely chopped

3 tablespoons bacon fat

2 cups red wine

*1 quart Lamb Stock (see Appendix) or
braising liquid from lamb shank*

METHOD Thoroughly sweat the onion, carrot, celery, and garlic in the bacon fat. Deglaze with the wine and reduce to a glaze. Add the stock or braising liquid and slowly reduce to about 1 cup, skimming constantly. (If braising liquid is used, this reduction cannot be made until the shank has finished cooking.) When you feel the consistency is right, strain. Serve warm.

Wine Notes

This would be a fabulous entrée for a cold winter's night, especially if accompanied by a lush, extracted, unfiltered, yet soft Cabernet Sauvignon — a comforting wine for a comforting dish. The creaminess of the nutty risotto will resolve any tannins that might seem to obstruct the wine's ability to merge with the garlicky-sweet meat, while being echoed by the rich oak tones of a Cabernet. Cabernet matured in American oak barrels makes a unique statement of vanilla and almost coconut nuances, such as in the great wines of Silver Oak Cellars (both the Napa Valley and the Alexander Valley offerings) and the heretofore unknown (but wonderful) Cedar Mountain in Livermore. Finally, this style of Cabernet often carries a dill or olive component, providing another dimension of flavor for the lamb.

Lamb Loin with Pickled Lamb's Tongue, Celery Root, Celery Juice, and Rosemary-Infused Lamb Stock Reduction

This dish features the fabulous combination of rich lamb's tongue, sweet lamb loin, and the clean taste of celery — an absolutely perfect trio. Serving a preparation like this is a great way to introduce people to lamb's tongue, an item some might normally shy away from.

Serves 4

1 12-to-14-ounce trimmed lamb loin

2 teaspoons olive oil

10 rosemary sprigs

1 medium celery root, peeled

About 2 cups Chicken Stock (see Appendix)

Salt and pepper

1 tablespoon grapeseed oil

1 cup celery leaves

Pickled Lamb's Tongues (see Appendix)

Rosemary-Infused Lamb Stock Reduction (recipe follows)

Celery Juice (see Appendix)

16 cloves Roasted Garlic (see Appendix)

METHOD Marinate the lamb loin for several hours in the olive oil and 6 sprigs of rosemary. Braise the celery root in Chicken Stock to cover for about 45 minutes, or until just soft in the center. Cool in the broth. Season the lamb loin with salt and pepper. Heat an ovenproof sauté pan over medium-high heat until it is quite hot, add the grapeseed oil, and sear the meat on all sides. Place the loin in a 450-degree oven for 3 to 5 minutes, turning over once, halfway through the cooking time. When the meat is just shy of medium-rare, remove it to a warm place and allow it to rest. It will continue to cook to a perfect medium-rare.

Heat a very little water in a sauté pan, and wilt the celery leaves slightly. Lightly season with salt and pepper. Cut the braised celery root and the lamb's tongues in ⅛-inch slices, place on a sheet pan, and warm in the oven for a few moments. Slice the lamb loin into approximately 16 slices.

ASSEMBLY On each plate, layer slices of lamb loin with the tongue, celery root, and wilted celery leaves. Drizzle a little Rosemary-Infused Lamb Stock Reduction and then some Celery Juice around the edges of the plates. Garnish with cloves of roasted garlic and remaining rosemary.

Rosemary-Infused Lamb Stock Reduction

½ cup Lamb Stock Reduction (see Appendix)

3 to 4 rosemary sprigs

METHOD Heat the Lamb Stock Reduction, steep the rosemary for about 45 seconds, and strain. Serve warm.

Wine Notes

The two lamb meats here are enhanced by a heady combination of garlic and rosemary, and the sweetness of the celery root. A berry-centered, slightly herbal red wine, such as a Pomerol or St.-Emilion, will support the lamb flavors while echoing the embellishments. A young Château La Dominique or Pavie-Decesse from a generous vintage like 1989 will work handsomely, as will a softer Château Le Bon Pasteur or Château Gazin.

Rack of Lamb with Vegetable Ragoût, Mustard Spätzle, and Mustard and Thyme Reduction

~~~~~~

*The meat on a rack of young spring lamb is so succulent that it virtually
disappears in your mouth. In this preparation the sweet, rich lamb is balanced
with a sharp edge of mustard, both in the sauce and in the spätzle.
The vegetables are a satisfying, earthy element that help make this a nicely rounded dish.*

Serves 4

2 trimmed racks of lamb

5 tablespoons olive oil

*2 tablespoons chopped, mixed herbs
(e.g., rosemary, thyme, etc.)*

*4 to 5 cups assorted seasonal vegetables
(e.g., beets, carrots, corn, mushrooms,
squash, peas)*

4 tablespoons butter

1 cup Vegetable Stock (see Appendix)

Salt and pepper

Mustard Spätzle (recipe follows)

*Mustard and Thyme Reduction
(recipe follows)*

Herb Oil (see Appendix)

METHOD Rub the lamb with 3 tablespoons
of olive oil, sprinkle with 1 tablespoon
herbs, and marinate overnight. Heat a large
ovenproof pan over medium-high heat, add
2 tablespoons of olive oil, and sear the lamb
on all sides. Transfer to a 450-degree oven
and roast for 8 to 12 minutes, depending on
the size of the racks and the desired degree
of doneness. Remove the racks when they
are a little underdone and allow them to
rest for 4 to 5 minutes. They will continue
to cook and the meat will have the chance
to *soften up.*

For the vegetable ragoût, peel and slice the
vegetables as appropriate. Combine 2 tablespoons of butter, Vegetable Stock, remaining herbs, and a little salt and pepper in a
pot and stew the vegetables for 2 or 3 min-

utes over medium heat until they are just
cooked through.

Just before serving, sauté the cooked Mustard Spätzle briefly in 2 tablespoons of butter to create a very desirable crispy effect.

ASSEMBLY Put a mound of vegetable
ragoût on each plate. Slice the rack into
chops and place 3 or 4 around the vegetables. (If desired, the meat can be cut off the
bone and sliced.) Drizzle the reduction
sauce around the edges. Sprinkle a small
amount of Herb Oil over the reduction
sauce and strew spätzle onto each plate
as well.

Mustard Spätzle

1 cup less 2 tablespoons all-purpose flour

2 tablespoons whole wheat flour

½ teaspoon salt

¼ teaspoon ground black pepper

1½ teaspoons stone-ground mustard

1½ teaspoons Dijon mustard

1 egg, beaten

½ to ¾ cup milk

METHOD In a mixing bowl, combine
everything but the milk. Add enough milk
to make a somewhat stiff batter. Cover the
dough, refrigerate, and let rest for 1 to 2
hours. To cook, drop ½ teaspoons of batter
from a spoon or pastry bag into simmering,
lightly salted water, or put the batter
through a colander or a special sliding
cutter designed for making spätzle. Cook
for about 1 minute or until done. Strain and
set aside.

Mustard and Thyme Reduction

1 onion, peeled and chopped

1 stalk celery, peeled and chopped

1 carrot, peeled and chopped

1 green bell pepper, seeded and chopped

1 tablespoon olive oil

1 tablespoon butter

2 cups red wine

4 quarts Lamb Stock (see Appendix)

2 tablespoons mustard seed

1 bunch thyme

METHOD In a medium sauté pan, sweat the
onion, celery, carrot, and pepper in the olive
oil and butter until they are just beginning
to brown. Deglaze with red wine and
reduce down to a glaze. Add the Lamb
Stock and the mustard seed and slowly
reduce to about 1 quart. Strain and continue to reduce to 1 cup. Steep the thyme in
the reduction for 40 seconds or so and
strain. Serve warm.

Wine Notes

In this classical preparation, the lamb dominates the flavor profile, though the mustard and thyme add a lively zip. A classical
wine seems in order as well, and none fits
the bill better than a mature Bordeaux.
A great Pauillac, such as Château Lynch-
Bages 1982 or Château Pichon-Lalande
1978, would be a fine accompaniment,
although many top-quality Napa Valley
Cabernets have achieved a stature of lovely
maturity. Examples include Château Mon-
telena 1978, Heitz *Martha's Vineyard*
1974, and Stag's Leap Wine Cellars "Cask
23" 1979.

Grilled Loin of Lamb with Roasted Fennel, Black Truffles, Sweet Corn Flan, and Sweet Corn Broth

This is a wonderful, delicate preparation of lamb that I often serve in June and July when truffles are in season. The roasted fennel provides an earthiness and the corn flan a sweet richness, so the dish is at once both light and luscious. The grilled loin, which acquires a subtle smokiness from the live fire, provides the ultimate satisfaction in what I think is a sublimely elegant combination of flavors.

Serves 4

1 fennel bulb

Olive oil

2 7-to-8-ounce trimmed baby lamb loins

Grapeseed oil

Salt and pepper

3 ounces black truffles, sliced (about 1 medium)

¼ cup shelled sweet peas, blanched and shocked

¼ cup sweet corn kernels, blanched and shocked

¾ cup Sweet Corn Broth (see Appendix)

Sweet Corn Flans (recipe follows)

Italian flat-leaf parsley

METHOD Rub the fennel bulb with a little olive oil and roast at 350 degrees for 1 hour or until thoroughly cooked and golden brown. Rub the meat with a little grapeseed oil and grill over a medium-hot wood fire on both sides until just shy of medium-rare. Season with salt and pepper on all sides, remove to a warm place, and allow to rest for 4 to 5 minutes. In the meantime, reheat the roasted fennel if necessary, and cut it into 12 or so slices. Heat the truffles, peas, and sweet corn kernels in the Sweet Corn Broth.

ASSEMBLY Place 3 slices of fennel in each bowl. Spoon the broth and vegetables into the bowls. Cut each lamb loin on a bias into 6 pieces, and place 3 slices in each bowl on top of the fennel. Place a corn flan in the center of each bowl and sprinkle with snipped Italian parsley.

Sweet Corn Flans

1 cup sweet corn kernels (2 ears corn)

¼ yellow bell pepper, chopped

2 teaspoons olive oil

½ teaspoon cumin

¼ teaspoon turmeric

½ cup heavy cream

3 large egg yolks

Salt and pepper

METHOD In a nonstick pan, sauté the corn and bell pepper in olive oil over medium heat until the vegetables are soft and translucent. Add the cumin and turmeric and continue cooking for a few minutes until the spices are thoroughly incorporated into the vegetables. Put the corn, cream, and egg yolks in a blender and purée. Season with salt and pepper and pass through a fine strainer, discarding the solids. Pour into 4 2-ounce timbale cups and cook for 30 to 40 minutes in a bain-marie at 300 degrees. Unmold just before serving.

Wine Notes

This preparation, which incorporates the flavors of sweet corn and earthy fennel in a very light broth, takes the lamb into another realm. The surrounding flavors call for a rich, heady Alsace Riesling, but the lamb itself demands red wine and its tannins. A soft, almost sweet style of Merlot, such as the Pride Mountain or Markham Napa Valley offerings, carries the combined sweetness of the young lamb, sweet corn, and roasted fennel, yet is light enough for this elegant preparation.

VARIETY MEATS

People are sometimes squeamish about eating variety meats (by variety meats I mean primarily organ meats such as liver and sweetbreads, but in this category I also include other items like lamb's tongue, tripe, oxtails, and pig's feet). All of these meats can be prepared in myriad ways with fantastic results. Frequently at the restaurant, I describe everything on the plate except the variety meat element hidden beneath a piece of meat or fish. Not until after my guests have finished the course will I reveal what made everything so incredibly delicious.

People today are very health-conscious, and consequently may be concerned about eating certain variety meats. Rather than eliminate these wonderful foodstuffs altogether, my solution is to serve them in very small amounts, or to use them as an accent in a preparation to highlight a specific meat or fish. You will note that I have used variety meats as such in a number of recipes in other parts of this book.

I love tripe and tongue and kidneys, not just the classics like sweetbreads or foie gras. And for something really different, there is monkfish liver, a wonderful delicacy that is favored in Japan, and is sometimes referred to as foie gras from the sea.

Veal Sweetbreads with Butternut Squash, Celery Root, Sweet Corn, and Veal Stock Reduction

*Ideally, sweetbreads should be prepared, as they are in this dish, so that they
are slightly crispy on the outside, but creamy and soft on the inside. I have also incorporated
butternut squash, celery root, sweet corn, and a little crisp bacon into this particular preparation.
The flavors form a straightforward, complementary backdrop for the sweetbreads,
but at the same time each is just assertive enough on its own to come across independently.
Additionally, braised Swiss chard adds an astringency that cuts nicely into the sweetbreads.
The Veal Stock Reduction contributes a necessary richness and the Celery Root Coulis
adds a further layer of depth to a most satisfying package.*

Serves 4

4 2- to 3-ounce sweetbread noisettes

3 cups Chicken Stock (see Appendix)

Salt and pepper

1 tablespoon grapeseed oil

1½ tablespoons unsalted butter

¼ cup diced butternut squash

¼ cup diced celery root

2 tablespoons sweet corn kernels

1 tablespoon bacon fat

2 tablespoons Sauternes

1 tablespoon crispy bacon

1 tablespoon chopped Italian flat-leaf parsley

*4 Swiss chard leaves, halved lengthwise,
center removed*

½ cup Veal Stock Reduction (see Appendix)

¼ cup Celery Root Coulis (recipe follows)

METHOD Gently poach the sweetbreads in Chicken Stock until medium-rare (about 8 minutes). Remove, clean off any membranes or veins, and lightly season with salt and pepper. In a heavy-bottomed sauté pan, sauté the sweetbreads in the grapeseed oil and ½ tablespoon of butter over medium heat for 5 to 6 minutes, turning them from time to time. In the meantime, sauté the butternut squash, celery root, and corn in the remaining butter and the bacon fat over medium-high heat, stirring frequently. Deglaze with Sauternes and let it evaporate away completely. This will effectively steam the vegetables to completion. Add the bacon and half the Italian parsley and season with salt and pepper. Blanch the Swiss chard for 10 seconds or so in boiling salted water. Quickly remove, drain, and season with salt and pepper.

ASSEMBLY Arrange 2 pieces of Swiss chard in the center of each plate. Spoon some of the vegetable mixture onto the Swiss chard. Cut each sweetbread *noisette* in half and place on a mound of vegetables. Drizzle 2 tablespoons of Veal Stock Reduction and 1 tablespoon of Celery Root Coulis onto each plate. Sprinkle with remaining chopped parsley.

Celery Root Coulis

1 cup peeled and cubed celery root

1 tablespoon unsalted butter

¼ to 1 cup Vegetable Stock (see Appendix)

Salt and pepper

METHOD Sweat the celery root in the butter over medium heat, stirring frequently for 12 to 14 minutes until it is thoroughly softened but not browned. Barely cover with Vegetable Stock and simmer for 10 minutes. Purée in a blender, adding additional Vegetable Stock if necessary. Strain through a fine strainer and season with salt and pepper. If too thin, reduce to the desired consistency.

Wine Notes

Creamy, rich sweetbreads, smoky bacon, and sweet celery and corn aromas and flavors need a high-extract, full-bodied foil in a red wine selection. A warm-climate ripe red from Provence or the southern Rhône in a rich year will fit in nicely. Grenache-based Châteauneuf-du-Pape or Gigondas will complement the dish perfectly.

Terrine of Foie Gras with
Mesclun, 100-Year-Old Balsamic Vinegar,
and White Truffle Oil

*This terrine is a marvelous way to begin a luxurious meal. It sets the tone perfectly,
and if you really want to go all out, you can add a little black truffle, and dress the greens with white truffle oil
and a very, very old balsamic vinegar. The sweetness of a very old balsamic vinegar is the
best friend foie gras has ever had — the older the balsamic vinegar, the sweeter and more complex the taste.
This is a nice make-ahead dish that can be sliced and served right at the last moment.
This is a very difficult preparation to give exact measurements for because so much depends on the size of the
terrine mold and the amount of fat that is rendered from the foie gras slices when they are seared.
I like to use a small 6-inch, 1-quart terrine mold, which should yield approximately 12 ½-inch slices.*

Serves 4

¼ to 1 lobe foie gras

Salt and white pepper

3 to 4 tablespoons Sautérnes

3 to 4 tablespoons brandy

1 bunch spinach leaves, cleaned
and stemmed

Oil for mold

2 or 3 roots salsify

2 cups loosely packed mesclun greens

8 teaspoons white truffle oil

8 teaspoons 100-year-old balsamic vinegar

8 teaspoons reduced Beet Juice
(see Appendix)

2 tablespoons julienned black truffles

Kosher salt and black pepper

METHOD Cut ¼-inch slices of foie gras from the lobe and devein them. Lightly season with salt and white pepper. Marinate in the Sauternes and brandy for several hours.

In a nonstick pan over medium-high heat, quickly sear the foie gras slices on both sides. Do not overcook. Cool the foie gras slightly on paper towels. Wilt the spinach leaves in the foie gras fat and blot on a paper towel. Season the spinach lightly with salt and pepper and allow to cool. Rub the terrine mold with a little oil and line it with plastic wrap. Arrange a layer of foie gras slices in the terrine, and top with a layer of spinach. Continue the layering process until the mold is filled. Press down and drain off any excess fat; cover and refrigerate for 2 to 3 hours.

Peel the salsify roots and slice them lengthwise with a vegetable peeler into 12 or 16 thin strips. Place the strips on a nonstick sheet pan or parchment paper and bake at 375 degrees until golden and crispy, about 5 or 6 minutes.

ASSEMBLY Cut ½-inch slices (or the desired thickness) of the foie gras terrine. Place a mound of mesclun greens in the center of each plate and top each with 2 slices of the terrine. Arrange the salsify around the terrine. Drizzle some white truffle oil and balsamic vinegar on the greens and around the plates. Drizzle some Beet Juice around the plate. Top the greens with the julienne of black truffle. Season with a little kosher salt and black pepper.

Wine Notes

The balsamic vinegar and white truffle oil provide the aromatic hooks in this lovely dish, while the foie gras provides an unforgettable rich flavor. A fine aromatic match might be an Alsace Gewürztraminer, but the slight bitterness of the variety can be unpleasant. The greens create a bitter balance all their own. A ripe Marsanne from California or even Australia would be the perfect flavor, with its honeysuckle fragrance and soft palate feel. Lou Preston's Dry Creek Marsanne is a great example in a restrained style, and Mitchelton, in Goulburn Valley, and Château Tahbilk, in Hunter Valley, make excellent honeyed Australian versions.

Seared Monkfish Liver
with Braised Endive, Lemongrass-Infused
YellowTomato Coulis, and Basil Oil

This rich organ meat benefits tremendously when paired with slightly astringent braised endive leaves.
The accents of tomato, basil, and lemongrass add complementary flavor components that
help to showcase the liver and give its one-dimensional flavor a little depth, without coming on too strong.
I frequently serve monkfish liver prepared in this — or a very similar — way, as an amuse gueule
(a tiny appetizer) in order to tantalize diners with something they would probably not order off the menu.
Because it is so exotic, it really attracts the guests' attention, and they almost always love it.

Serves 4

2 large heads Belgian endive

3 to 4 cups Chicken Stock (see Appendix)

4 2-ounce pieces of monkfish liver
(foie gras or duck liver could be substituted)

2 teaspoons grapeseed oil

2 teaspoons unsalted butter

Salt and pepper

Lemongrass-Infused Yellow Tomato Coulis
(recipe follows)

Basil Oil (recipe follows)

2 tablespoons yellow tomato concassée

1 teaspoon lemongrass, finely cut on the bias

1 teaspoon chopped parsley

METHOD Place the heads of endive in a deep saucepan with enough Chicken Stock to cover, and cook over low heat for 1 hour. Cut each lengthwise into 12 to 14 thin strips and set aside. Sauté the monkfish liver in grapeseed oil and butter over medium-high heat for approximately 1½ to 2 minutes on each side or until the liver is nicely browned but just medium-rare. Season with salt and pepper. In a small saucepan, warm the Lemongrass-Infused Yellow Tomato Coulis. Reheat the braised endive strips in a 400-degree oven for 3 or 4 minutes. Season with salt and pepper.

ASSEMBLY Place 6 or 7 strips of braised endive on each plate. Arrange the pieces of monkfish liver on top of the endive. Spoon a tablespoon or so of Lemongrass-Infused Yellow Tomato Coulis onto each plate Drizzle a little Basil Oil onto each plate, then strew the tomato *concassée*, lemongrass strands, and parsley around the plate.

Lemongrass-Infused
Yellow Tomato Coulis

1 tablespoon chopped shallots

1 teaspoon chopped garlic

2 tablespoons chopped lemongrass,
tied in cheesecloth

2 teaspoons olive oil

1 cup yellow tomato concassée

Salt and pepper

Tomato Water (optional) (see Appendix)

METHOD Sweat the shallots, garlic, and lemongrass sachet in olive oil over very low heat for 12 to 14 minutes. Add the tomatoes and continue to cook for 10 minutes. Remove the sachet and blend the mixture for 20 seconds. Pass it through a fine mesh sieve and season with salt and pepper. If the coulis is too thick, it can be thinned to the desired consistency with Tomato Water.

Basil Oil

1½ cups packed basil leaves, rinsed

½ cup packed Italian flat-leaf parsley, rinsed

1½ cups grapeseed oil

½ cup olive oil

METHOD Blanch the herbs in boiling, salted water, then immediately shock in cold water and drain. Roughly chop the herbs, squeeze out the excess water, and place in the blender with enough oil to cover. Purée well, add remaining oil, and pour into a container. Refrigerate for 2 days, strain through a fine mesh sieve, refrigerate 1 more day, and decant.

Wine Notes

The delicate Asian flavors here seem to find natural alliances in wine: lemongrass is a typical component of Sauvignon Blanc, and basil occurs in several white as well as red wines. A crisp, light wine with a nod to these flavors should kick off a meal well. La Jota Viognier, a rather lean, austere version of the variety, will echo the lemongrass while supporting the sea flavors of the monkfish liver.

Tartlet of Braised Tripe and Blood Sausage with Mustard-Sauternes Sauce and Red Wine Reduction

While tripe is generally not considered to be part of the fine dining repertoire, I believe that when it is properly prepared it can be a complex and delicious meat. The flaky pastry holds all of the wonderful elements that make up the tartlet, including heady blood sausage, mushrooms, and root vegetables, along with the star, the braised tripe. (You can find blood sausage in many ethnic butcher shops.) The Mustard-Sauternes Sauce brings an almost sweet-and-sour effect to the rich ingredients, and the intense Red Wine Reduction serves to tie together all the varied intense flavors and textures of this dish, while at the same time cutting through them.

Serves 4

12 ounces tripe

3 cups Chicken Stock (see Appendix)

⅔ cup unsalted butter

8 baby turnips, cooked and peeled

8 Chiogga beets, cooked and peeled

⅓ cup hon shei meji mushrooms

⅓ cup tiny hedgehog mushrooms

Salt and pepper

½ cup spinach, cleaned and stemmed

1 cup cooked and cubed blood sausage

Mustard-Sauternes Sauce (recipe follows)

Red Wine Reduction (see Appendix)

4 4-inch pâte brisée tartlet shells (recipe follows)

METHOD Braise the tripe in Chicken Stock and ½ cup of butter over very low heat for 4 to 5 hours or until it is very soft. Cool it in the liquid, then cut it into 1½ x ½-inch strips. Reserve ¼ cup of the braising liquid. Cut the turnips and beets into quarters. Sauté the mushrooms in 2 tablespoons of butter over medium heat until just soft, about 4 to 6 minutes, and season with salt and pepper. In a medium sauté pan, carefully wilt the spinach in 2 teaspoons of butter over medium heat until it is just barely cooked, about 2½ minutes. In a large sauté pan, warm the tripe in 3 or 4 tablespoons of the braising liquid. Fold in the root vegetables and mushrooms and stir carefully for 2 minutes. Add the blood sausage and stir carefully again, as the sausage will break up very easily. Fold in the wilted spinach and season with salt and pepper.

METHOD Spoon 2 or 3 tablespoons of the Mustard-Sauternes Sauce onto the center of each plate, and top with a tartlet shell. Fill each tartlet with some of the tripe mixture and drizzle a little of the Red Wine Reduction around the edges of the plate.

Pâte Brisée

1 cup flour

¼ teaspoon kosher salt

¼ teaspoon cracked black pepper

1½ teaspoons sugar

4 tablespoons butter

1 egg yolk

1½ teaspoons lemon juice

1 tablespoon ice water

METHOD In a food processor, process the flour, salt, black pepper, sugar, and butter for 30 to 40 seconds. Add the yolk, lemon juice, and ice water and pulse until just combined. Refrigerate for at least 1 hour before using.

Mustard-Sauternes Sauce

4 medium shallots, peeled and chopped

1½ tablespoons unsalted butter

4 tablespoons white wine

⅔ cup Sauternes

2 cups Chicken Stock (see Appendix)

2 to 3 tablespoons Dijon mustard

METHOD Sweat the shallots in the butter over low heat until thoroughly softened, about 3 to 4 minutes. Deglaze with the white wine and reduce down to a glaze. Deglaze with the Sauternes and reduce down to about 2 tablespoons. Add the Chicken Stock and slowly reduce down by about one third. Purée and return to the pan. Bring to a boil and whisk in 2 to 3 tablespoons of mustard, depending on the desired taste.

Wine Notes

A spicy, somewhat fruity white wine will do battle with the Mustard-Sauternes Sauce in this dish, while allowing the delicate flavor of the slowly cooked tripe to melt in the mouth, but the vegetable components, especially the mushrooms and beets, will work better with a light red wine. The striking Müller-Catoir wines, intensely mineral and dry, make excellent white companions, and focused younger Piemontese reds complement the earthy flavors nicely. Good red selections would include Nebbiolo d'Alba or Freisa from Giacomo Conterno.

Seared Squab Liver with Crispy Beets, Pig's Feet, Spinach, and Port Wine Reduction

Squab liver is a little more interesting than duck liver: the flavor is more subtle and the texture is a touch more delicate. In this preparation, the finely julienned and lightly fried beets not only add a nice sweetness, which benefits most liver preparations, but they also provide the perfect textural foil to the butterlike liver. The braised and crisped pig's feet add an interesting textural contrast as well, but they also give heartiness to the dish. The spinach creates a cleansing effect which is important for rich foods like the liver and pig's feet. Finally the Squab Stock Reduction Sauce ties everything together with a satisfying richness.

Serves 4

8 squab livers
1 tablespoon unsalted butter
¼ cup Crispy Pig's Feet (see Appendix)
¼ cup finely julienned beets
1 cup grapeseed oil
Salt and pepper
8 tiny squash
12 spinach leaves, cleaned and stemmed
Port Wine Reduction Sauce (recipe follows)

METHOD Sauté the squab livers in the butter over medium-high heat until browned on all sides but still underdone in the middle, about 2 minutes. Crisp up the pig's feet in a nonstick pan over medium heat for 4 to 5 minutes. Carefully fry the beets in the grapeseed oil until they are cooked through and crispy. Remove them to a paper towel and season with salt and pepper. Blanch the squash in boiling, salted water for a minute or so. Remove to a cutting board, cut into wedges, and season with salt and pepper. Blanch the spinach leaves.

ASSEMBLY Arrange the squash pieces in a fan shape in the center of each plate. Lay 3 pieces of spinach on each of the plates. Slice each of the squab livers into 3 or 4 pieces and lay them on top of the squash. Strew the pig's feet around the edges of the plate. Place some of the fried beets on top of the liver and drizzle a couple tablespoons of Port Wine Reduction Sauce around the edges of the plate.

Port Wine Reduction Sauce

2 tablespoons chopped onion
2 tablespoons chopped celery
2 tablespoons unsalted butter
½ cup port wine
2 tablespoons balsamic vinegar
2 cups Chicken Stock (see Appendix)

METHOD Sweat the onion and celery in the butter over medium heat until softened and translucent. Deglaze with the port wine and slowly reduce to a glaze. Deglaze with the balsamic vinegar and reduce to a glaze. Add the Chicken Stock and slowly reduce by half, skimming away any fat or impurities. Strain and slowly continue to reduce to the desired consistency, about ⅓ to ½ cup of sauce.

Wine Notes

The richly flavored liver demands an assertive, medium- to full-bodied red wine, and the beet flavors seem to reflect the sweetness of a fine Burgundy. A mature Grand Cru, such as Clos de Tart 1986 or Bonnes-Mares de Vogue 1978, would work majestically, although there is room to argue for a younger, more heady wine. The great 1990 Burgundies provide a wide choice, especially in Pommard Premier Cru from Courcel and Lejeune.

GRAINS

I use grains frequently at the restaurant, both as the primary component of a dish and as a backdrop to other foods. In fact, I use quinoa so much, it has almost become one of my signature foods. Sometimes I prepare this exceptional grain with vegetables only, and other times I use it to accompany meats, or as a base for game birds or organ meats. Most of the grains I use can be found in the average supermarket. The more exotic ones, such as quinoa and amaranth, are readily available in health food stores. One of the advantages of working with grains is that most can be prepared in advance and reheated at the last moment. I generally cook them with water rather than stock, as stocks can be overpowering to most grains' delicate flavor.

Each type of grain has its own distinctive characteristics. Quinoa, for instance, combines the best features of couscous and barley: it is crumbly yet chewy, with a wheaty, nutty flavor—very complex, and very versatile. Amaranth, another wonderful grain, is slowly gaining recognition as a delicious, healthful food. It, too, is similar in texture to couscous and barley, but it is somewhat denser. It has a wonderful richness, with a subtle corn flavor and hints of hazelnuts.

Amaranth with Duck Confit, Sweet Corn, and Truffle Sauce

*I think that amaranth is a greatly under-appreciated grain. While many
other grains have made headway into the culinary scene, the interesting and complex
amaranth inexplicably has not. Its dense texture provides a unique heartiness,
and, interestingly, the flavor reminds one of sweet corn, hazelnuts, and wheat all rolled into one.
I find that amaranth nicely highlights particularly flavorful foodstuffs, such as black truffles,
while still retaining an identity of its own. I created this dish to showcase the grain,
primarily, but it would be easy enough to picture a larger portion of duck, or any other meat,
and a smaller amount of the amaranth, depending on your desires.*

Serves 4

2 cups cooked amaranth

½ cup sweet corn kernels

1 tablespoon bacon fat, butter, or duck fat

*1 cup loosely packed washed and stemmed
spinach leaves*

1 tablespoon butter

*1 tablespoon water or Chicken Stock
(see Appendix)*

3 tablespoons grapeseed oil

*2 thighs of Duck Confit, all bones removed
(recipe follows)*

*3 tablespoons Foie Gras Butter
(see Appendix)*

Truffle Sauce (recipe follows)

Salt and pepper

METHOD Warm the amaranth in a stainless-steel bowl over boiling water, stirring
from time to time with a wooden spoon.
Lightly sauté the sweet corn in bacon fat,
butter, or duck fat until just cooked, and
remove to a paper towel. In a medium sauté
pan over medium-high heat, melt 1 tablespoon of butter into the tablespoon of water
or Chicken Stock. Toss in the spinach and
thoroughly wilt, while stirring constantly.
Remove the wilted spinach from the pan to
a cutting board and chop finely.

In a small nonstick sauté pan, heat the
grapeseed oil until very hot, but not to the
smoking point. Place the duck thighs in the
hot oil, skin side down, and reduce the heat
to medium. Cook for 1½ minutes or so until
crispy, then turn and cook for 45 seconds or
until warmed through. Remove to a paper
towel and keep warm. Fold the corn, spinach, and Foie Gras Butter into the amaranth and season with salt and pepper. Cut
each duck thigh in half.

ASSEMBLY Spoon some of the amaranth
into the center of each of 4 warm plates. If
you desire a cleaner, more precise shape, you
can use a cutter or a timbale mold. Place a
piece of duck on the amaranth and drizzle 1
to 2 tablespoons of Truffle Sauce around it.

Duck Confit

8 duck thighs, barely trimmed, bones left in

6 tablespoons kosher salt

1 tablespoon sugar

1 tablespoon coarsely ground black pepper

1 tablespoon garlic, peeled and sliced

2 teaspoons chopped ginger

6 cups rendered duck fat

METHOD Rub the duck thighs with kosher
salt, sugar, black pepper, garlic, and ginger.
Pack tightly in a small container and cover
with plastic wrap. Allow to marinate for
72 hours in the refrigerator, turning the
thighs over every 12 hours. When ready to
cook, thoroughly rinse the marinade off
the thighs. Place the thighs in a heavy-
bottomed pot, cover with duck fat, and
bake covered with foil at 180 degrees for
about 4 hours or until the meat is quite soft
but still has some body left to it. Cool and
store in the fat until ready to use.

Truffle Sauce

½ cup peeled and chopped onion

½ cup peeled and chopped celery

2 cloves garlic, peeled and chopped

2 teaspoons bacon fat

¼ cup red wine

1 quart Chicken Stock (see Appendix)

2 tablespoons chopped black truffle

METHOD In a medium saucepan over a
medium heat, sweat the onion, celery, and
garlic in the bacon fat until thoroughly
softened but not quite golden. Deglaze with
the wine and reduce to a glaze. Add the
Chicken Stock and slowly reduce by half,
skimming away any impurities and fat that
may rise to the surface. Pass the sauce
through a strainer and continue to reduce
slowly down to about ½ cup or to the
desired consistency. Just before serving,
add the chopped truffles and simmer for
30 seconds.

Wine Notes

Although the tiny grain is rather delicate
here, the focus of the wine accompaniment in this case should be for the rich
Duck Confit. The boisterous brashness of
a Côte Rôtie, especially of Guigal's 1989
Côtes Brune et Blonde, adds a peppery
gaminess to the dish while not being so
tannic that it dominates, and the ripeness
of the wine freshens the palate with
each sip.

Arkansas Short-Grain Rice with Peeky Toe Crab, Fennel, and Sun-Dried Tomatoes with Japanese Pear Juice and Chicken Stock Reduction

The best word that I can use to describe Arkansas short-grain rice is toothsome.
In fact, it is so delicious and earthy, it is hard to stop yourself from eating and eating.
In this preparation I have added the sweet elements of crab, fennel, pear, and sun-dried tomatoes
which nicely accentuate the soft, nutty quality of the rice. As for the crab,
I prefer the variety from Booth Bay Harbor, Maine, as it seems particularly sweet. However,
red rock crab, Dungeness crab, or any lump crab would all work well as substitutes.

Serves 4

1 cup cooked Arkansas short-grain rice (in water or stock)

⅓ cup finely diced zucchini

2 tablespoons butter

¼ cup julienned fennel

½ cup thoroughly cleaned Peeky Toe crab meat

2 ½ tablespoons peeled and finely julienned oil-packed sun-dried tomatoes

¼ cup peeled and finely chopped Japanese pear

2 teaspoons finely chopped parsley

Salt and pepper

8 tablespoons Chicken Stock Reduction (see Appendix)

4 tablespoons Japanese Pear Juice (recipe follows)

1 Japanese pear, cut into Parisienne balls or small pieces

METHOD Warm the rice in a stainless-steel bowl over boiling water. Meanwhile, lightly sauté the zucchini in 1 tablespoon of butter over low heat until just softened. Remove to a paper towel. Sauté the fennel in 1 tablespoon of butter over low heat, stirring frequently, until it is lightly caramelized. Remove to a paper towel. Using a wooden spoon, fold the crab, zucchini, 1 tablespoon of sun-dried tomatoes, and chopped Japanese pear into the grain and mix thoroughly. Fold in the parsley and season with salt and pepper. Warm the Chicken Stock Reduction and the Japanese Pear Juice in separate saucepans.

ASSEMBLY Place a mound of rice in the center of each plate (use a 2-ounce timbale mold if a cleaner shape is desired), and top each with a little fennel. Drizzle 2 tablespoons or so of the Chicken Stock Reduction and about 1 tablespoon of Japanese Pear Juice around each mound of rice, and garnish the plate with the Parisienne balls and remaining sun-dried tomatoes.

Japanese Pear Juice

1 Japanese pear

METHOD Peel, seed, and juice the pear. Bring to a gentle boil and reduce it by half, skimming along the way.

Wine Notes

An earthy, dry Riesling from Alsace, or a Halbtrocken from the Mosel will flatter the nutty qualities of the grain here, while merging seamlessly with the sweet crab-meat and the fruit element of pear. Zind-Humbrecht's Rangen de Thann Grand Cru Riesling brings a pleasing fruity, earthy pungency to the palate. On the slightly sweeter side, Selbach-Oster's Zeltinger Schlossberg Riesling Kabinett will be a welcome accompaniment.

White and Yellow Grits
with Spring Vegetables and Chervil

~~~~~~

Grits are seldom associated with fine dining or a grand meal, but why not?
Dressed up and elegantly presented, grits are as versatile and as interesting as couscous or quinoa,
and I particularly love its porridgelike texture. This particular preparation sings of
spring with delicate baby fennel, buttery fava beans, toothsome green onions, and an aromatic,
poetic, chervil-infused tomato broth. When I eat something like this, it never enters my mind that it is
vegetarian. Instead, I think of it as soul-satisfying food that is, for me, almost spiritual.

Serves 4

*4 tablespoons unsalted butter
(or bacon or duck fat)*

*1 cup cooked yellow grits
(2 cups water, 6 tablespoons grits)*

*4 tablespoons blanched and chopped
green onions*

*3 tablespoons chopped Roasted Red Bell
Pepper (see Appendix)*

*1 cup cooked white grits
(2 cups water, 6 tablespoons grits)*

3 tablespoons yellow or red tomato concassée

Salt and pepper

12 baby fennel bulbs

4 tablespoons olive oil

20 pearl onions, unpeeled

40 to 60 fava beans (about ½ pound)

1½ cups Tomato Water (see Appendix)

¼ cup chopped chervil

12 whole green onions

Chervil sprigs for garnish

METHOD Stir 1 tablespoon or so of butter into the just-cooked yellow grits. If the grits are still too stiff, add a little stock or water. Fold in 2 tablespoons of chopped green onion and the roasted bell pepper. Heat the white grits in the same manner, stirring in 1 tablespoon of butter, then the remaining chopped green onions and tomatoes. Season both mixtures with salt and pepper.

Rub the baby fennel bulbs with 2 tablespoons of olive oil and roast them at 400 degrees for 20 minutes, turning occasionally, until they are just caramelized and thoroughly cooked. Remove from the oven and season with salt and pepper.

Toss the pearl onions in the remaining 2 tablespoons of olive oil and roast them in the oven at 400 degrees for 15 minutes or until softened. Remove from the oven, remove the skins, and season lightly with salt and pepper. Shell the fava beans and blanch them in boiling salted water for 45 seconds or so, then shock them in cold water. Remove the little sheath of skin from each bean.

Heat the Tomato Water to a boil, add the chopped chervil, and steep for 20 seconds. Strain and return to the heat and bring to a boil. Add the whole green onions and poach for a moment. Add the fennel, pearl onions, and fava beans and heat them through. Stir in the remaining 2 tablespoons of butter and season with salt and pepper.

ASSEMBLY Using a cutter or ring, form 2 timbales on each plate, one of white grits, and one of yellow. Arrange the vegetables evenly around them. Spoon on the broth-like sauce and sprinkle with fresh chervil.

Wine Notes

The slight sweetness of corn, amplified by the roasted fennel and pearl onions, make this delicious preparation difficult to pair with wine. All of the flavors are delicate, yet need some support from a wine of lively acidity. *R* de Ruinart Champagne, with its Chardonnay base, provides a creamy, elegant counterpoint to the vegetable and grain flavors. The effervescence of a sparkling wine also plays well texturally.

Lobster Basmati with Guava and Macadamia Nut Coulis

When I prepare basmati rice, my first inclination is to pair it with something tropical — guava, mango, or macadamia nuts, for example. The wonderful nutty quality of this particular grain seems to beg some sweet addition. In this preparation, besides the tropical influences, I introduce a little lobster, which adds a richness to the aromatic rice. A bit of caviar is in order if you wish to be unconditionally extravagant.

Serves 4

1¼ cups cooked basmati rice

¼ cup cooked chopped lobster meat plus 4 whole shelled claws

2 teaspoons chopped mint

¼ cup roasted macadamia nuts, chopped

2 tablespoons peeled and finely chopped red onion

1 tablespoon dark sesame oil

Salt and pepper

1 tablespoon melted butter

⅓ cup Guava Coulis (recipe follows)

¼ cup Macadamia Nut Coulis (recipe follows)

1 to 2 ounces Osetra caviar (optional)

METHOD In a stainless-steel bowl set over boiling water, warm the basmati rice, stirring with a wooden spoon. Fold in the chopped lobster meat, mint, macadamia nuts, and red onion, and mix well. Add the sesame oil and season with salt and pepper. Rub the lobster claws with a little of the melted butter, set them on a plate with 1 tablespoon of water, and place in a 450-degree oven for 60 seconds to reheat.

ASSEMBLY Spoon 2 tablespoons or so of the Guava Coulis into the center of each plate. Using a rectangular cutter (or any other shape you desire), place a mound of basmati rice on the Guava Coulis. Drizzle a little of the Macadamia Nut Coulis around the edge of the Guava Coulis. (This can easily be accomplished with a squeeze bottle.) Place a warm lobster claw on each mound of rice. If you are using caviar, put a little on each claw.

Guava Coulis

3 guavas, peeled and cut up

2 teaspoons butter

2 teaspoons sugar

¼ to ½ cup water

METHOD Sweat the guava pieces in butter over low heat, stirring frequently until softened. Stir in the sugar and cook for 30 seconds or so. In a blender, purée with enough water to attain the desired consistency, and strain.

Macadamia Nut Coulis

½ cup macadamia nuts

2 tablespoons grapeseed oil

¼ to ½ cup water

Salt and pepper

METHOD Roast the macadamia nuts in a 250-degree oven for 20 minutes, or until the desired color (the longer they are roasted, the darker and more richly colored the coulis). In a small blender, process the nuts with the oil and enough water to create a smooth purée. Season to taste with salt and pepper.

Wine Notes

This pretty dish is light and refreshing, and will be well matched with a wine that reinforces these attributes. The delightful nutty/fruity balance that results from the interplay of macadamias and guava will be echoed by a firm yet fruity Riesling from the Rheinhessen or the Pfalz. The liveliness of the pepper and mint combination, along with the somewhat jarring element of red onion, balance the sweet lobster meat, and also argue for a low-alcohol, flavorful, dry Riesling such as Lingenfelder Grosskarlbacher Osterberg Spätlese Halbtrocken (Pfalz) or Merz Ockenheimer Laberstall Spätlese Trocken (Rheinhessen). The addition of caviar moves the flavor profile to a much richer wine. If you utilize this option, look at a Grand Cru Riesling from Alsace or a classical Mosel Spätlese from J. J. Prüm or Dr. Thanisch.

Pearled Barley with Roasted Apple, Foie Gras, Rhubarb, and Ginger-Apple Reduction Sauce

One of the most enjoyable things about barley is its incredible chewy texture, which is very much like al dente pasta, but somewhat more delicate and flavorful. In this preparation, the barley can play either a bigger or smaller role, depending on how much you want to feature it. For example, bigger pieces of foie gras and apple can be used, or they could be pared down to practically nothing. That is the beauty of a spontaneous cuisine.

Serves 4

1 cup cooked pearled barley

6 1½-ounce slices of foie gras, cleaned

1 Granny Smith apple, skin on and cored

¼ cup peeled and diced rhubarb

1½ cups apple juice

2 tablespoons julienned rhubarb

2 tablespoons julienned apple

½ cup Ginger-Apple Reduction Sauce (recipe follows)

Salt and pepper

1 tablespoon chopped parsley

METHOD Warm the barley in a stainless-steel bowl over hot water. Cut 2 pieces of foie gras into a small dice, to match the diced rhubarb. In a nonstick pan over low heat, sauté the diced foie gras pieces until just medium rare, then remove them to a paper towel in a warm spot, leaving the fat in the pan. Cut 4 ⅛-inch-thick *rings* of apple, and season with salt and pepper. Turn the heat up slightly and brown the apple slices, about 3 or 4 minutes on each side. Remove them to a paper towel. Discard any remaining fat. In the meantime, in separate saucepans, poach the diced rhubarb in 1 cup of apple juice and the julienned rhubarb in the remaining ½ cup of apple juice for 3 or 4 minutes or until the rhubarb just softens and the natural sweetness of the apple juice takes the raw tang out of the rhubarb. Stir the diced rhubarb, diced foie gras, and about 1 tablespoon of Ginger-Apple Reduction Sauce into the barley. Season to taste with salt and pepper. In a medium sauté pan, sear the slices of foie gras until just browned and still medium rare, about 20 to 30 seconds on each side. Remove them from the pan to a cloth or paper towel, and season with salt and pepper.

ASSEMBLY Lay a slice of seared foie gras in the center of each plate. Spoon a little mound of barley on the foie gras. If a cleaner shape is desired, use a timbale mold or cutter slightly smaller than the piece of foie gras. Place a slice of apple on top of the barley. Spoon a little more barley around the edges of the plate, and arrange the julienned apple and julienned rhubarb around the plate and on top of the apple. Drizzle 2 tablespoons of Ginger-Apple Reduction Sauce onto each plate and sprinkle on a little parsley.

Ginger-Apple Reduction Sauce

2 tablespoons peeled and chopped onion

2 teaspoons peeled and chopped ginger

2 tablespoons chopped apple

1 tablespoon dark sesame oil

3 tablespoons mirin

3 cups Chicken Stock (see Appendix)

Salt and pepper

METHOD Sweat the onion, ginger, and apple in the sesame oil over medium heat until the ingredients are well softened but not yet browned, stirring frequently. Deglaze with the mirin. Add the Chicken Stock and slowly reduce by half, skimming off any fat or impurities that may rise to the top. Strain and continue to reduce down to ½ cup. Season with salt and pepper.

Wine Notes

Whereas most of Charlie Trotter's foie gras preparations are intended as red wine dishes, here is an occasion to serve Sauternes. The use of apple and ginger adds a sweet spiciness to the already rich barley, whose creamy yet firm texture begs for a wine of some substance. A sweet Sauternes will take this combination over the hedonistic edge, while not overwhelming the palate if this is a middle course in a grand meal. Try Château Guiraud 1983 or Château Rieussec 1986.

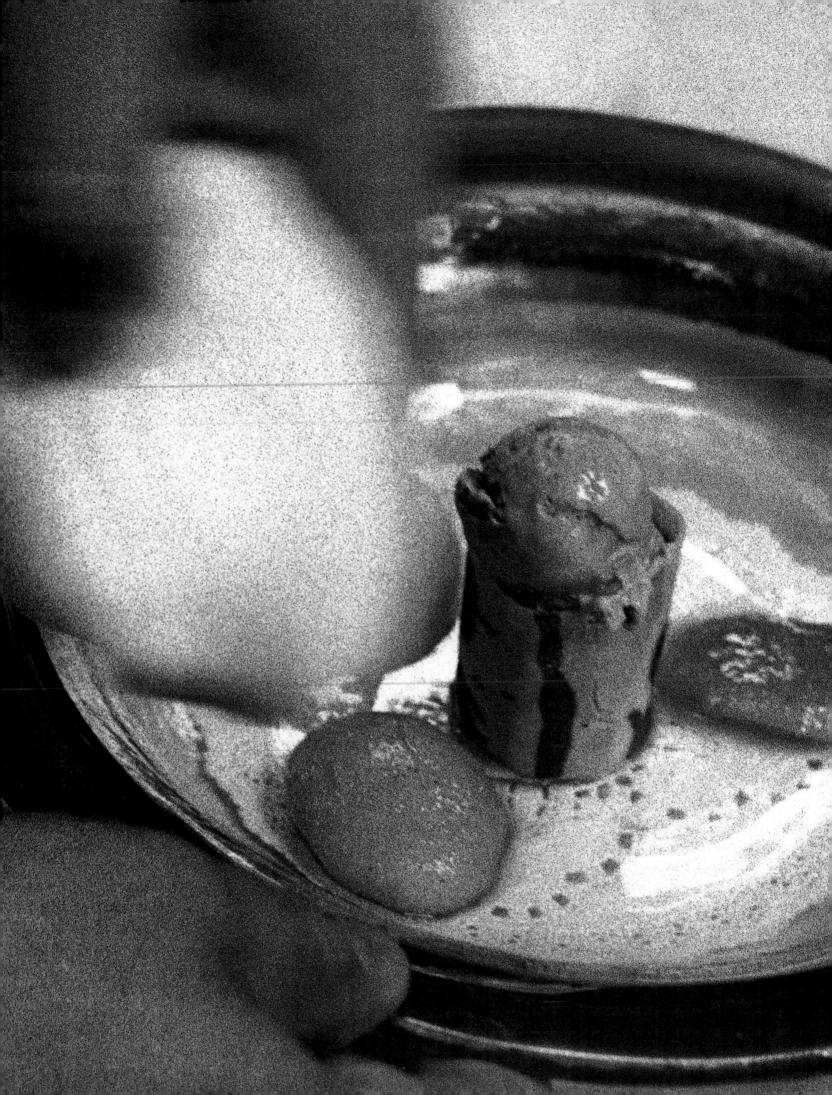

DESSERTS

---◆◆◆---

For the most part, I like to emphasize fresh seasonal fruits in my desserts. After all, there is no reason why desserts cannot be healthy as well as hedonistic. Besides, some of the really great dessert wines, such as late-harvest Rieslings, Sauternes, and Barsac are classic accompaniments for compositions that include fruits such as apricots and peaches.

Of course, there are times when nothing will do but something outrageously rich, so on occasion there will be desserts on the menu that break all my rules. But rich or light, I like to build complex contrasts into my desserts. In one, a warm fruit syrup comes in contact with a bit of cool ice cream; in another, a sensuous custard is set off by a crisp pastry. I also love hot and cold elements paired together.

I approach the dessert station like the rest of the areas of the kitchen: everything is made to order, and served the moment it is ready.

Warm Liquid-Center Chocolate-Banana Bread Pudding with Malt Ice Cream

Sometimes there is no better way to end a feast than with a dessert that is uncompromisingly laden with chocolate. This dessert features one of my favorite flavor combinations: chocolate and bananas. Not only is there a chocolate sauce and a chocolate-banana bread pudding, but each serving of the pudding has a filling of warm liquid chocolate. The malt ice cream that accompanies it is an extra fillip that pushes the whole creation over the edge.

Serves 12

8 tablespoons butter, softened
½ cup brown sugar
½ cup granulated sugar
2 eggs
1¼ cup mashed ripe bananas (about 3 bananas)
2 cups flour
1 teaspoon baking soda
½ teaspoon salt
Chocolate Custard (recipe follows)
Chocolate Ganache (recipe follows)
Bittersweet Chocolate Sauce (recipe follows)
Coconut-Caramel Wafer (recipe follows)
Malt Ice Cream (recipe follows)

METHOD Cream the butter and sugars using the paddle attachment on a mixer. Beat in the eggs one at a time, scraping the bowl often. Add the mashed bananas and mix to combine. Sift together the flour, baking soda, and salt, and gradually beat this into the butter mixture. Divide the dough into 2 greased and floured loaf pans about 6 x 2½ inches and bake at 350 degrees for 40 to 45 minutes. Allow to cool. (The bread can be baked in one larger loaf pan, but increase the cooking time by 5 or 10 minutes.)

To make the pudding, trim away all the outer crust of the banana breads and cut the loaves into cubes. Place the cubes in a large bowl and pour in enough Chocolate Custard to cover them. Cover with plastic and allow to stand at room temperature for 30 minutes. The bread should soak up most of the custard.

Butter 12 2-inch round rings and place them on a parchment-lined sheet pan. Densely pack the molds about halfway with banana bread. Place a ball of the ganache in the center of each ring, pack in more banana bread to cover the ganache, and spoon on a little more custard. (If custard seeps out the bottom, do not worry.) Bake at 375 degrees for 12 to 15 minutes or until the pudding is set. Remove from oven and allow to rest for 5 minutes.

ASSEMBLY Place a little pool of Bittersweet Chocolate Sauce in the center of each plate. Unmold the bread puddings and place one in the center of each plate. Place a Coconut-Caramel Wafer on top of each pudding and top with a scoop of Malt Ice Cream.

Chocolate Custard

⅔ cup heavy cream
½ pound bittersweet chocolate
¼ cup butter, cut into pieces
2⅓ cups milk
3 eggs plus 2 egg yolks
¼ cup brown sugar

METHOD Bring the cream to a boil and pour it over the chocolate and butter. Mix until melted and smooth. Combine in a saucepan with the milk and place over medium heat, stirring until everything has combined thoroughly. Remove from heat. Put the eggs, yolks, and sugar in a stainless steel bowl and whisk together. Pour the warm chocolate mixture into the egg mixture, whisking constantly. Pass through a fine mesh sieve.

Chocolate Ganache

¼ cup plus 2 tablespoons heavy cream
2 tablespoons granulated sugar
1 tablespoon butter
½ pound bittersweet chocolate, chopped

METHOD Combine the cream and sugar in a small saucepan and bring to a boil. Pour over the butter and chocolate. Stir until completely melted and smooth. Strain and refrigerate until set. After chocolate has set, roll ganache into 12 ½-inch balls. Refrigerate until ready to assemble. (Extra ganache can be formed into balls and dipped into cocoa powder to make chocolate truffles.)

Bittersweet Chocolate Sauce

2 cups heavy cream
¼ cup granulated sugar
2 tablespoons butter
½ pound bittersweet chocolate, chopped

METHOD Combine the cream and sugar in a small saucepan and bring to a boil. Pour over the butter and chocolate. Stir until completely melted and smooth, and pass through a fine mesh sieve. If made ahead, reheat in a double boiler before serving.

Coconut-Caramel Wafer

½ cup butter
½ cup granulated sugar
½ cup toasted shredded fresh coconut
Pinch of salt
5 tablespoons flour
2 tablespoons heavy cream

METHOD Put the butter, sugar, coconut, and salt in a saucepan over low-medium heat and mix constantly until the butter is completely melted. Make sure the butter does not separate from the rest of the ingredients. Remove from heat. Add the flour

and mix it in thoroughly. Add the cream, and mix well. Place 12 small mounds of wafer batter on a nonstick sheet pan, and smooth each into a 2-inch circle. Bake at 350 degrees until lightly browned. Remove from oven and cool. The batter can be made ahead of time and refrigerated until ready to use.

Malt Ice Cream

(This recipe may yield extra ice cream, but it will keep well in the freezer.)

12 egg yolks

¾ cup granulated sugar

2 cups heavy cream

2 cups half-and-half

⅓ cup barley malt powder*

METHOD Combine the egg yolks and sugar in a bowl. Bring the cream and half-and-half to a boil and pour it over the yolk mixture. Place back on the heat and stir constantly until thick enough to coat the back of a spoon. Cool over an ice bath. Add the barley malt powder, strain through a fine mesh sieve, and freeze in an ice machine.

* If barley malt powder is unavailable, liquid barley malt can be substituted. Mix 3 tablespoons of the liquid with the egg yolks and sugar and proceed with the recipe.

Wine Notes

This sweet chocolate dessert has a pure, childlike appeal. It is extremely difficult to match with wine. Only a bold, concentrated, even tannic fortified wine will do, such as a young, single-quinta Porto. The Quinta do Vesuvio 1990 expresses the concentrated berry and pepper qualities of young vintage port, yet seems more accessible. The berry aromas and flavors dovetail nicely with chocolate, and the tannins seem to balance the chocolate's sweet intensity. It works even better than a glass of milk!

Nancy Silverton's Panna Cotta with Oven-Dried Fruits and Fruit Coulis

The first time I tasted this custard dessert, I thought it was so wonderful that I just had to reproduce it. I called Nancy Silverton at Campanile in Los Angeles, and she generously gave me the recipe to her incomparable creation. The eggless custard itself is almost lighter than air, and ethereal with the perfume of vanilla. The oven-dried fruits add a stunning, concentrated natural fruit flavor, but the coup de grâce comes from the crispy, wafer-thin pastry beneath the custard. This remains one of my all-time favorite desserts!

Serves 6

1¼ leaves gelatin or 1¼ teaspoons granulated gelatin

1½ cups heavy cream

½ cup milk

4 tablespoons sugar

2 vanilla beans

6 Pastry Circles (recipe follows)

Oven-Dried Fruits and Fruit Coulis (recipe follows)

METHOD Soften the gelatin in cold water. Combine the cream, milk, and 1 tablespoon of sugar in a saucepan. Split the vanilla beans and scrape in the seeds. Bring to a boil, watching carefully and stirring, and gently boil for just under 1 minute. Remove from heat and whisk in the remaining sugar and the gelatin until it is dissolved. Line a fine mesh strainer with several layers of cheesecloth and strain the mixture through it to remove the vanilla seeds. Chill over ice until cool to the touch but not set up. Stir, then pour it into 6 ⅓-cup fluted tart tins (nonstick ones work the best). Refrigerate for about 45 minutes. To speed up the process, put them in the freezer for 15 minutes, but do not allow to freeze.

ASSEMBLY Dip the bottom of each tin in warm water for about 15 seconds, top with a pastry circle, invert onto your hand, and gently place in the center of a plate. Pour a little of each coulis in 4 spots around the panna cotta and place the corresponding dried fruit in each. Serve immediately.

Pastry Circles

1½ cups flour

9 tablespoons cold butter, cut in small pieces

½ teaspoon sugar

½ teaspoon salt

½ cup ice water

METHOD Sift the flour and cut the butter into the flour. Add the sugar and salt and mix with hands until combined. Pour in the cold water and mix just until the dough begins to come together. Wrap in plastic wrap and allow to rest in a cool place for 30 minutes. Flour a working surface and roll the dough to ¹⁄₁₆-inch thickness, making it as even as possible. With a pastry cutter, cut 6 circles that correspond to the size of the tart tins. Line the back of a sheet pan with parchment and place the circles on top. Top with another piece of parchment and another sheet pan, so that the pans are back to back. Put a heavy, ovenproof weight on the top pan, perhaps a brick wrapped in foil. Bake at 350 degrees for 15 minutes or until evenly browned. Cool to room temperature.

Oven-Dried Fruits and Fruit Coulis

2 bananas, peeled
1 cup black cherries
1 papaya
10 strawberries
½ pineapple
6 figs
Water or Simple Syrup (optional)
(see Appendix)

METHOD Prepare each fruit as necessary (peel, pit, core, etc.). Cut 18 slices ¹⁄₁₆-inch thick of each fruit (cut 9 cherries in half). Place on nonstick pans and bake at 220 degrees for approximately 1½ hours until dried.

For the coulis, purée the remaining fruits separately, slowly adding enough water or Simple Syrup to create the desired consistency and sweetness, but allowing the pure fruit flavor to come through. Any extra purée could be used for sorbets.

Wine Notes

The dominant flavor of the eggless flan itself is vanilla, which pairs nicely with a dessert wine that has been affected by botrytis, the *noble rot* so prized by sweet wine producers. When this characteristic combines with the acidity of a Sauternes or Barsac, the flavors of the various dried fruits come forth as well. Try Château Coutet 1986, or for a more earthy experience, the Château Lafaurie-Peyraguey 1982.

Peach and Crème Brûlée Napoleon with Green Tea Crème Anglaise and Peach Juice

I always have some sort of custard dessert on the menu, and over the years, crème brûlée has appeared on many occasions. This particular version came to be because I wanted to serve a crème brûlée that was a bit unusual. Certainly the creamy custard is present, but the crispy pastry and delicate bits of sweet peach make for added interest and complexity. The ultimate touch is the exotic Green Tea Crème Anglaise, which pushes the whole thing into another zone.

Serves 4

3 egg yolks plus 2 whole eggs
3 to 4 tablespoons granulated sugar
1½ cups heavy cream
½ vanilla bean
3 large ripe peaches
Phyllo Squares (recipe follows)
6 mint leaves, cut into a fine chiffonade
Green Tea Crème Anglaise (recipe follows)

METHOD Whisk the 3 egg yolks and 1 tablespoon sugar together in a bowl. Put ¾ cup cream in a pan; split the vanilla bean, scrape the seeds into the cream, and add the pod. Bring just to a boil, then slowly pour the hot cream into the yolks, whisking constantly. Return the mixture to the pan and continue stirring over heat for 1 minute. Pour the mixture from the pan into a bowl, remove the vanilla bean, and set the mixture aside. Whisk together the 2 whole eggs and 1 tablespoon sugar, stir in ¾ cup cream, and set aside.

Peel the peaches and remove the pits. Cut one into ¼-inch dice and another into at least 36 ¹⁄₁₆-inch slices. For the peach juice, cut the third peach into quarters, purée, strain through a fine mesh sieve, and reserve. Oil the bottom of an 8 x 8-inch pan and line it with plastic wrap. Evenly distribute the diced peaches in the pan. Whisk together the two egg mixtures, and pour it over the diced peaches, making sure it reaches to the edges of the pan. Bake at 250 degrees until firm (about 25 to 35 minutes). Refrigerate until cool, then place in the freezer for about 20 minutes. Invert onto the back of a sheet pan, remove the plastic wrap, and cut into 2-inch squares. Sprinkle with 1 to 2 tablespoons granulated sugar, and caramelize under the broiler. (At the restaurant, we use a blow torch.)

ASSEMBLY Place a square of crème brûlée in the center of each plate and top each square with 2 slices of peach and then a phyllo square. Repeat the process and continue until the napoleons are stacked 4 layers high. Cut the remaining peach slices into strips and mix with the mint leaves, and use this as a garnish. Drizzle alternately with Green Tea Crème Anglaise and peach juice. Serve immediately.

Phyllo Squares

2 9-inch-square sheets of phyllo
1 to 2 tablespoons melted butter
1 tablespoons confectioners' sugar

METHOD Place a piece of parchment on an inverted sheet pan. Put 1 sheet of phyllo on the paper, brush with melted butter, sprinkle with confectioners' sugar, and top with a second sheet of phyllo. Cut into 16 2¼-inch squares. Place a second sheet pan on top of the napoleons and weight it with a brick or other heavy, ovenproof object. Bake at 375 degrees until lightly browned (10 to 12 minutes).

Green Tea Crème Anglaise

3 egg yolks
¼ cup sugar
1 cup plus 2 tablespoons milk
2 tablespoons heavy cream
1 tablespoon green tea powder

METHOD Whisk the egg yolks and sugar together until smooth. Combine the milk, cream, and green tea powder in a saucepan

and bring to a boil. Pour the hot mixture into the egg yolks, whisking continuously. Return the mixture to the saucepan and cook over medium heat, stirring constantly, until it thickens just enough to coat a spatula. Do not allow the mixture to boil. Pass through a fine mesh strainer and set aside.

Wine Notes

In this dessert, the intense peach flavors are balanced by the exotic astringency of a tea-infused sauce. It is best paralleled by a wine whose intensity of sweetness is matched by its firm acidity and some spicy characteristics. Alois Kracher's Zwischen den Seen wines from Austria are magnificent examples of this style. His Scheurebe Beerenauslese 1991 contains the right firmness to let the fruit flavors of the dish come forward, and a slightly peppery quality that adds to the experience. While rather sweet, this wine is marvelously balanced, and quite clean.

Crispy Quinoa Pudding with Pine Nuts, Carrot Sorbet, and Gingered Carrot Coulis

Compared to a true rice pudding, this quinoa pudding is considerably lighter. It is also more flavorful, bolstered as it is by the nutty quality of the quinoa, which has much more of a presence than its rather bland cousin. With the addition of carrot, this dessert displays a unique combination of flavors and textures. The carrot aspect is inspired by Middle Eastern pastries in which carrots are used for their natural sweetness, reducing the need for sugar or honey. The ginger adds the perfect final touch, both binding together and accentuating the grain and the carrot.

Serves 6

2 cups cooked quinoa

½ cup Vanilla Crème Anglaise (recipe follows)

1 egg

2 tablespoons quinoa flour or all-purpose flour

¼ cup dried blueberries (dried cherries also work well)

5 tablespoons roasted pine nuts

1 tablespoon peanut oil

1 to 2 tablespoons butter

18 slices Candied Carrot (recipe follows)

Carrot Sorbet (recipe follows)

Gingered Carrot Coulis (recipe follows)

METHOD Thoroughly combine the quinoa, Vanilla Crème Anglaise, egg, flour, blueberries, and 4 tablespoons of pine nuts.

Pack the quinoa mixture into 6 buttered 2- to-2½-inch round rings or cutters. Heat the peanut oil in a nonstick sauté pan. Place the filled molds in the hot pan and cook on both sides until lightly browned, about 2 minutes on each side. One or 2 teaspoons of butter may be added to facilitate browning. Place in a 350-degree oven for 5 minutes.

Remove from oven and run a wet knife around the edges of the molds to loosen the pudding.

ASSEMBLY Place 3 slices of Candied Carrot in the center of each plate and top with a timbale of quinoa pudding. Place 2 or 3 scoops of Carrot Sorbet around each timbale, and drizzle Gingered Carrot Coulis around each. If a richer effect is desired, drizzle a little Vanilla Crème Anglaise around the plate as well. Garnish with a few roasted pine nuts.

Vanilla Crème Anglaise

(This recipe makes more than you need, but it is difficult to make a smaller portion.)

4 egg yolks

¼ cup sugar

1 cup milk

½ vanilla bean

1 teaspoon brandy (optional)

METHOD Whisk the yolks with the ¼ cup of sugar for 20 seconds or so. Place the milk in a saucepan, split the bean, and scrape the seeds into the pan. Bring to a boil, then reduce the heat and allow to simmer for 3 to 5 minutes so the vanilla flavor saturates the milk. Whisk the hot milk into the yolk mixture, then return it to the heat. Stir constantly with a wooden spoon until the sauce thickens enough to coat the back of the spoon. Strain immediately into a container, and submerge in an ice bath. If desired, add brandy when cooled.

Candied Carrot

1 cup Simple Syrup (see Appendix)

8 paper-thin lengthwise slices of carrot (use a mandolin or a vegetable peeler)

2 cups peanut or grapeseed oil

METHOD In a medium saucepan, bring the Simple Syrup to a boil. Add the carrot slices and reduce the heat to medium. Cook for 15 minutes or until slices are somewhat transparent. Remove them from the syrup and place them on a screen to drain and cool. Heat the oil to 325 degrees. Carefully drop the carrot slices into the hot oil. They will sink to the bottom briefly, then sizzle a bit and rise. When the sizzling action begins to taper off, the slices are done. Remove them from the oil immediately and drain on a screen or mesh cooling rack. As they cool, separate and lay them flat to harden.

Carrot Sorbet

1 cup fresh carrot juice, strained
Grind of black pepper
½ cup sugar

METHOD Combine ingredients and freeze in an ice cream machine.

Gingered Carrot Coulis

¼ teaspoon cornstarch
¼ cup fresh carrot juice, strained
Sprinkle of salt
Grind of black pepper
1 teaspoon chopped ginger

METHOD Mix the cornstarch with 1 tablespoon of carrot juice. Heat the remaining juice and season gently with salt, pepper, and ginger. Stir in the cornstarch mixture and whisk over heat till slightly thickened. Rewarm before serving if desired.

Wine Notes

The nutty flavor of the grain is extended by the pine nuts, and fuses beautifully with the sweetness of blueberries and the carrot sorbet, which is quite sweet. A very sweet wine is in order, perhaps in the 15–20 percent residual sweetness range. The rare and exotic Tokaji Aszú *6 Puttonyos*, Hungary's greatest contribution to the world of wine, picks up the sweetness level that the Carrot Sorbet establishes, and makes a fascinating, nearly syrupy statement in its own right. You might also consider a sweet late-harvest Riesling from California or Washington; Navarro, in Anderson Valley, makes an occasional sweet wine that can be decadent, and Kiona, in the Yakima Valley, has made some wonderful Beerenauslese-style Rieslings that would work well here.

Warm Quince Soup with Fruit Sorbets and Oven-Dried Apples

Serving a hot soup with a chilled sorbet creates a wonderful sensation in the mouth. This combination can be enjoyed year around—simply use the fruits that are in season. In this version, there are three different sorbets, and I have added oven-dried apple slices and a delicate little fruit salad as a textural element. Most of the guests at the restaurant sample one of my fruit soups after their final savory course; they have always met with huge success.

Serves 4

1 quince (about 1 pound),
peeled and coarsely diced
¼ cup peeled and diced apple
¼ cup diced pineapple
2 cups water
¼ cup sugar
1 star anise
2 tablespoons peeled and finely diced Japanese pear
2 tablespoons peeled and finely diced papaya
2 tablespoons peeled and finely diced kiwi
Kiwi Sorbet (recipe follows)
Papaya Sorbet (recipe follows)
Prickly Pear Sorbet (recipe follows)
Oven-Dried Apples (recipe follows)

METHOD For the soup, bring the quince, apple, pineapple, water, and sugar to a boil. Remove from the heat, add the star anise, cover, and let steep for 30 minutes. Remove the star anise, purée, and strain. Warm just before serving. To make the fruit salad, combine the pear, papaya, and kiwi, and set aside.

ASSEMBLY Spoon a small mound of fruit salad into each bowl. Place a small scoop of each sorbet on the mound of fruit. Top with a few apple chips, and pour a little warm quince soup into each bowl.

Kiwi Sorbet

4 kiwi, peeled
½ cup Simple Syrup (see Appendix)
Lemon juice, as needed

METHOD Purée the kiwi and Simple Syrup in a blender. Strain and taste for balance. If the mixture seems too sweet, add a few drops of lemon juice. Freeze in an ice cream machine.

Papaya Sorbet

1 ripe papaya, peeled, seeded, and diced
¼ cup Simple Syrup (see Appendix)
Lemon juice, as needed

METHOD Purée the papaya and Simple Syrup in a blender. Strain and taste for balance of flavors, adding a little lemon juice if needed. Freeze in an ice cream machine.

Prickly Pear Sorbet

10 prickly pears
½ cup Simple Syrup
Lemon juice, as needed

METHOD Cut the pears in half and scoop out the pulp. Purée the pulp and Simple Syrup in a blender. Strain and taste for balance of flavors, adding a little lemon juice if needed. Freeze in an ice cream machine.

Oven-Dried Apples

1 Granny Smith apple

METHOD Peel the apple and cut it into paper-thin slices. Trim into wedge shapes. Lay the slices out on a nonstick sheet pan and bake at 200 degrees for 50 to 60 minutes or until thoroughly dry.

Wine Notes

This refreshing and light dessert presents a high degree of acidity to match with wine. Most late-harvest wines are too sweet to work with the tartness of the sorbets, so the best wine will be a demi-sec Champagne. This type of wine will contain enough sweetness to meet the sweetness of the fruit without overwhelming it, and will set up the palate for a more substantial dessert or dessert wine later. Furthermore, it is not as aggressively effervescent as typical brut styles. The favorite recommendation is Veuve Clicquot Demi-Sec; Schramsberg Crémant will work if you prefer a fine American sparkler.

A Study in Apricot

*I devised this dish a few years ago for a special meal that I prepared with Roger Vergé
at the Masters of Food and Wine event in Carmel, California. Being paired with the legendary
Chef Vergé, a true culinary hero of mine, was one of the greatest moments in my culinary life,
and so I felt a desire to create a dessert that would be a true tour de force. The dessert was to be served
with the Wehlener Sonnenuhr Riesling Auslese Gold Cap 1983, a J. J. Prüm, brought by
Dr. Manfred Prüm. I devised a veritable meditation on the apricot, or what I called A Study in Apricot.
If time does not allow you to prepare every aspect of this elaborate dessert, one or two
of the elements would easily suffice as an elegant finish to any meal.*

Serves 6

Apricot Strudel (recipe follows)
Apricot Ravioli (recipe follows)
Tuiles *(recipe follows)*
Fruit Compote (recipe follows)
Apricot Ice Cream (recipe follows)
Grilled Apricot (recipe follows)
Apricot Sorbet (recipe follows)
Apricot Linzer Tart (recipe follows)
Apricot Sauce (recipe follows)
1 tablespoon mint leaves, finely julienned

METHOD Most of the components for this dish can be prepared ahead of time, but the final steps require a bit of coordination, so it would be best to have some assistance at that point. Preheat the oven to 375 degrees and have boiling water ready for the ravioli. Bake the Apricot Linzer Tart and Apricot Strudel for 8 to 12 minutes (one may be done before the other.) Reheat the Grilled Apricot halves in a 350-degree oven for 4 to 5 minutes. When the strudel and tart are almost done, boil the ravioli. Using a serrated knife, cut the tart into 1-to-1½-inch-wide strips. With the same knife, cut the strudel with alternating straight and angled cuts (like sushi) into 6 pieces also at 1-to-1½-inch increments. Warm up the Apricot Compote in a little saucepan.

ASSEMBLY Place a piece of strudel on each plate. Spoon some of the warm Apricot Compote onto the plate, place a *tuile* on each mound of compote, then fill each with more compote. Place a ravioli on each *tuile*. Do not be afraid to let some of the warm compote juice run out. Place a scoop of ice cream and a grilled apricot half on each plate, and top with a scoop of Apricot Sorbet. Lay down a piece of warm linzer tart and spoon a couple tablespoons of Apricot Sauce onto each plate. Garnish with a bit of mint.

Apricot Strudel

⅔ cup dried apricots
⅛ cup dried cranberries
½ cup water
1 tablespoon cognac
½ tablespoon chopped Preserved Ginger (see Appendix)
1 sheet phyllo dough
2 tablespoons butter
2 tablespoons confectioners' sugar

METHOD Coarsely chop the apricots and combine with the cranberries, water, cognac, and Preserved Ginger. Simmer for 5 minutes. Cool to room temperature. Strain any excess liquid (it can be used for sauce around the edges of the plate). Spread out the sheet of phyllo. Brush it very lightly with butter, sprinkle with the powdered sugar, and fold it in half lengthwise. Brush lightly with butter. Starting about an inch away from the edge of the longer side, spoon the apricot filling in a straight line all the way across the phyllo. Roll the strudel as tightly as possible, pressing out any air pockets along the way. Place on a nonstick sheet pan. Brush the top lightly with melted butter. Refrigerate until the final assembly.

Apricot Ravioli

6 apricots, peeled, pitted, and coarsely chopped
2 tablespoons water
1 tablespoon granulated sugar
¼ teaspoon ground black pepper
1 cup semolina flour
1 egg

1 tablespoon mint leaves, finely julienned
Egg wash

METHOD Place the apricots, water, and sugar in a saucepan and simmer for 10 minutes or until the apricots are thoroughly softened and the water has just evaporated. Pass the mixture through a food mill and season with black pepper. It should be fairly thick. If not, return it to the saucepan and stir over heat to evaporate excess moisture. Cool thoroughly. Process the flour and egg in a food processor until well combined. A couple of drops of water or a little more flour may be necessary to attain the perfect texture. Remove the dough from the machine and knead it until a ball is formed and it is uniform in texture. Allow the dough to rest for 1 hour.

Roll about ¼ of the dough through the pasta machine until you have reached its thinnest setting. Lay the sheet of pasta out on a lightly floured surface, and mist ½ of it with water. Quickly lay out the mint leaves in a single layer on the dry side. Fold the pasta in half and smooth it out. Beginning with a larger setting, carefully roll the pasta through the machine, and rework it down to almost the finest setting, being careful not to rip the pasta. Roll pasta into a sheet approximately 12-to-15-inches long. If the pasta has any tears in it, fold it in half and run it through the machine again.

Brush egg wash on half the sheet of pasta. On the dry side, spoon 6 small mounds of apricot purée, about 1 teaspoon each, approximately 1 inch apart. Fold the pasta in half, and firmly press it down around the edges of the purée to press out any air pockets. With either a small fluted pastry cutter or a round unfluted cutter about 1½ to 2 inches in diameter, cut out the ravioli. Squeeze edges firmly and refrigerate until ready to use. Refrigerate remaining dough for another use.

Tuiles

¼ cup granulated sugar
5 tablespoons flour
3 egg whites
5 tablespoons melted butter
Pinch of salt

METHOD Combine the sugar and flour, then stir in the egg whites and melted butter. Chill for 30 minutes. Cut a ¾ x 5-inch rectangle out of the center of a piece of cardboard. Place it on a nonstick sheet pan. Spread a tablespoon or so of the *tuile* mixture in the opening. Remove the cardboard and bake at 350 degrees for 8 to 10 minutes. When the *tuile* is just turning golden and beginning to set, quickly remove it from the oven and shape it into a square or round by wrapping it around a cutter or other mold. Repeat until you have 6 nice *tuiles*. Once you have mastered the technique, you can make 2 or even 3 at a time, but you must work quickly to mold them before they harden.

Fruit Compote

½ cup water
¼ cup granulated sugar
1-inch piece of vanilla bean
6 apricots, peeled, pitted, and cut into thin wedges

METHOD Put the water and sugar in a pan. Split the vanilla bean and scrape the seeds into the pan. Bring to a boil, add the apricot slices, and simmer for 1½ minutes. Strain, reserving both the liquid and the apricots. Purée about ¼ of the apricots back with the liquid. Combine all, and keep chilled until ready to use.

Apricot Ice Cream

⅔ cup puréed apricot
6 egg yolks
⅔ cup plus 1 tablespoon granulated sugar
3 cups heavy cream
2 tablespoons cognac
4 tablespoons finely chopped, peeled apricots

METHOD Heat the puréed apricot, slowly reduce by half, and cool. Stir together the egg yolks, ⅔ cup sugar, and apricot purée. Bring the cream just to a boil, then slowly pour it into the yolks, whisking constantly. Return the mixture to the pan and cook over medium heat, stirring constantly with a wooden spoon until the custard just thickens. Remove from heat and strain. Cool and freeze in an ice cream machine. In the meantime, dissolve 1 tablespoon of sugar in the cognac in a small pan. Add the chopped apricots and cook for 2 to 3 minutes over medium-low heat until the cognac evaporates and the apricots soften. Fold the apricots into the finished ice cream and freeze again until ready to use.

Grilled Apricot

3 medium apricots, peeled, halved, and pitted
2 tablespoons melted butter

METHOD Rub the apricots with the melted butter and slowly grill on both sides over low heat until the apricots are just softened and hot all the way through. (If a grill is unavailable, you can roast the apricot halves for about 10 minutes in a 350-degree oven.) Before serving, reheat in a 350-degree oven for 4 or 5 minutes.

Apricot Sorbet

5 ripe apricots, peeled and pitted
½ cup water
2 tablespoons Sauternes
¼ cup granulated sugar

METHOD Put all the ingredients in a blender and purée. Strain through a fine strainer and freeze in an ice cream maker until ready to use.

Apricot Linzer Tart

½ cup roasted almonds
½ cup confectioners' sugar
1 small egg white plus 1 whole egg
½ cup butter, softened
½ teaspoon vanilla extract
⅛ teaspoon salt
¼ cup flour
½ cup hazelnuts, roasted and ground
Egg wash
Pastry Cream (recipe follows)
4 apricots, peeled and pitted

METHOD For the dough, combine the almonds and confectioners' sugar in a food processor and completely pulverize. Add the egg white and butter and process to a smooth paste. Add the whole egg and process for 10 to 15 seconds. Scrape down the sides, add the vanilla and salt, and process for 5 to 10 seconds. Remove the dough from the machine and refrigerate for 1 hour before using.

Lightly sprinkle the work surface with flour. Roll the dough into a 10 x 5-inch rectangle ¼ inch thick. If the dough is difficult to handle, it can be rolled between 2 pieces of plastic wrap. If it becomes too soft, refrigerate for a few minutes before continuing. Trim the dough to 9 x 4 inches and transfer to a nonstick sheet pan. Cut two ½ x 9-inch strips and two ½ x 3-inch pieces from the scraps. Brush a little egg wash along the edges of the rectangle, then lay the strips of dough along its length and width, using the egg wash as a sort of glue. Refrigerate for 20 to 30 minutes. Spread some Pastry Cream in the center of the tart. Slice the apricots into eighths. Halve the slices widthwise and stand each piece, point up, in the pastry cream. It should be densely covered. Refrigerate until ready to bake.

Pastry Cream

2 egg yolks
⅓ cup granulated sugar

2 tablespoons cornstarch
1 cup milk
¼ vanilla bean

METHOD Combine the egg yolks, sugar, and cornstarch in a bowl. Put the milk in a small saucepan, split the vanilla bean, and scrape the seeds into the pan. Bring the milk to a boil, then slowly pour it into the yolks, whisking continuously. Return the mixture to the saucepan over medium heat and whisk constantly until it begins to boil. Boil gently for 1 minute, continuing to whisk. Strain, cover with plastic wrap, and cool.

Apricot Sauce

4 apricots, peeled, pitted, and quartered
4 tablespoons Sauternes
2 tablespoons sugar
1 tablespoon finely minced Preserved Ginger (see Appendix)
1 tablespoon water

METHOD Thoroughly purée all of the ingredients in a blender. Strain through a fine strainer and set aside.

Wine Notes

This majestic dessert demands a majestic wine, either a Sauternes or a late-harvest German Riesling. There are so many facets to the apricot motif in this dessert that it is nearly impossible to complement them all with one wine, so choose a wine of classic greatness such as Château d'Yquem 1959 or Wehlener Sonnenuhr Trockenbeerenauslese J. J. Prüm 1971, which are even more intense than the wine for which the dish was originally prepared. They are advanced to perfect, honeyed maturity, while still expressing the exciting acidity that makes them nearly immortal wines.

APPENDIX

Stocks and Broths

Chicken Stock

Yield: About 1½ quarts

15 pounds chicken bones
2 onions, peeled and chopped
2 carrots, peeled and chopped
4 stalks celery, peeled and chopped
1 head garlic, cut in half
1 celery root, peeled and chopped

METHOD Place the chicken bones and vegetables in a large pot. Cover with cold water (about 5 quarts) and bring to a boil. Lower the heat and simmer for 4 hours, skimming away any impurities that rise to the top. Strain and reduce to about 1½ quarts.

Lamb Stock: Follow the recipe for Chicken Stock, but substitute 15 pounds of lamb bones for the chicken bones, roasting the bones until browned before putting them in the stock pot. Add 1 cleaned and chopped fennel bulb and 1 seeded and chopped red bell pepper along with the other vegetables.

Rabbit Stock: Follow the recipe for Chicken Stock, but substitute 15 pounds of rabbit bones for the chicken bones, roasting the bones until browned before putting them in the stock pot. Add 2 chopped tomatoes along with the other vegetables, and simmer 2 hours.

Squab Stock: Follow the recipe for Chicken Stock, but substitute 15 pounds of squab bones for the chicken bones, roasting the bones until browned before putting them in the stock pot.

Veal Stock: Follow the recipe for Chicken Stock, but substitute 15 pounds of veal bones for the chicken bones, roasting the bones until browned before putting them in the stock pot.

Fish Stock

Yield: About 1½ quarts

10 pounds fish bones (sea bass, red snapper, or similar types work well)
4 tablespoons unsalted butter
2 stalks celery, chopped
1 onion, peeled and chopped
1 leek, peeled and chopped

6 cloves garlic, peeled and halved
2 cups white wine

METHOD Sauté the fish bones in butter for 5 minutes. Place in a large pot with the vegetables and the wine. Cover with cold water and bring to a boil. Simmer for 30 minutes, skimming away any impurities that rise to the top. Strain through cheesecloth and reduce to about 1½ quarts.

Vegetable Stock

Yield: About 1½ quarts

2 leeks, cleaned and chopped
4 Spanish onions, peeled and chopped
6 stalks celery, chopped
1 celery root
2 carrots, peeled and chopped
2 red bell peppers, seeded and chopped
1 rutabaga, peeled and cut up
1 fennel bulb, peeled and cut up
6 tomatoes, chopped
1 pound button mushrooms, cleaned
2 heads garlic, cut in half
2 parsnips, peeled and cut up

METHOD Place the vegetables in a large pot. Cover with cold water and bring to a boil. Simmer for 1 hour, skimming away any impurities that rise to the top. Strain and reduce to about 1½ quarts. Note: Vegetables may be deleted or substituted, depending on the flavor desired.

Blond Vegetable Stock: Use 6 leeks, 4 Spanish onions, 8 stalks of celery, and 2 celery roots and follow the method above.

Sweet Corn Broth

Yield: 3 cups

20 ears sweet corn, kernels removed
1 tablespoon unsalted butter
Salt and pepper

METHOD Cover the corn kernels with cold water by 2 inches or so. Bring to a boil, then simmer for 1 hour. Strain and slowly reduce to about 3 cups. Whisk in the butter, and season to taste with salt and pepper.

Wild Mushroom Stock

Yield: 1 cup

¼ cup peeled and chopped onion

6 cloves garlic, peeled and coarsely chopped
1 tablespoon butter
1 tablespoon olive oil
1½ pounds assorted wild mushrooms, thoroughly cleaned and coarsely chopped
3 cups water

METHOD Sweat the onions and garlic in the butter and olive oil until they just begin to caramelize. Add the mushrooms and sauté over medium heat for 6 to 8 minutes until they are just softened. Add the water and simmer for 25 minutes, skimming away any fat and impurities along the way. Strain through a fine strainer and slowly reduce to 1 cup.

Reduction Sauces and Consommés

Chicken Stock Reduction

Yield: ½ cup

3 tablespoons chopped fennel
1 tablespoon bacon fat or butter
½ cup red wine
¼ cup tomato concassée
3 cups Chicken Stock (see recipe above)

METHOD Sweat the fennel in the bacon fat over medium heat in a 1-quart saucepan until thoroughly softened. Deglaze with the red wine and reduce to a glaze. Add the tomato, then the Chicken Stock, and slowly reduce by half, skimming away any fat or impurities that may rise to the top. Strain, return to heat, and continue to reduce slowly to ½ cup or the desired concentration.

Rabbit Stock Reduction

Yield: ½ cup

2 tablespoons chopped smoked bacon
⅓ cup peeled and chopped carrots
⅓ cup peeled and chopped onion
⅓ cup peeled and chopped celery
2 cloves garlic, minced
1 cup red wine
3 cups Rabbit Stock (see recipe above)
6 sage leaves

METHOD In a medium sauté pan, slowly render the fat from the bacon. Add the carrot, onion, celery, and garlic and sweat thoroughly. Deglaze with red wine and reduce to a glaze. Add the Rabbit Stock and slowly reduce by half, frequently skimming away any impurities that rise to the top. Strain and continue to reduce to ½ cup or to the desired concentration. Steep the sage leaves in the reduction for 45 seconds and remove.

Lamb Stock Reduction

Follow the recipe for Rabbit Stock Reduction, substituting Lamb Stock for the Rabbit Stock, and omitting the sage leaves.

Squab Stock Reduction

Yield: ½ cup

⅓ cup peeled and chopped carrot
⅓ cup peeled and chopped onion
⅓ cup peeled and chopped celery
⅓ cup peeled and chopped red bell pepper
2 cloves garlic, peeled and minced
2 tablespoons olive oil
2 tablespoons sherry wine vinegar
½ cup white wine
¼ cup chopped tomato
3 cups Squab Stock (see recipe above)
Thyme or tarragon (optional)

METHOD In a medium sauté pan, sweat the carrots, onion, celery, red pepper, and garlic in olive oil until soft and translucent. Deglaze with sherry wine vinegar and reduce to a glaze. Add the white wine and reduce to a glaze. Add the tomato and Squab Stock and slowly reduce by half, frequently skimming any impurities that rise to the top. Strain and continue to reduce to ½ cup or the desired concentration. If desired, steep a few sprigs of thyme or tarragon in the reduction for 45 seconds, then remove.

Veal Stock Reduction

Yield: ½ cup

2 tablespoons peeled and chopped shallots
2 teaspoons peeled and chopped garlic
2 teaspoons butter
½ cup red wine
3 cups Veal Stock (see recipe above)
15 tarragon leaves, slightly chopped

METHOD Sweat the shallots and garlic in butter until thoroughly softened. Deglaze with the red wine and reduce to a glaze.

Add the Veal Stock and reduce by half, skimming away any fat or impurities that may rise to the top. Strain and continue to reduce slowly to ½ cup or to the desired concentration. Steep the tarragon in the reduction for 30 seconds, then strain.

Red Wine Reduction

Yield: ½ cup

1 small onion, peeled and chopped
1 stalk celery, peeled and chopped
6 cloves garlic, peeled and chopped
1 small red bell pepper, peeled and chopped
1 tablespoon bacon fat or olive oil
2 small tomatoes, chopped
½ cup balsamic vinegar
2 tablespoons port wine
1 bottle Cabernet Sauvignon or Zinfandel

METHOD Sweat the onions, celery, garlic, and red bell pepper in bacon fat or olive oil over low heat until thoroughly softened. Add the tomatoes, balsamic vinegar, and port and reduce to a glaze. Add the wine and slowly reduce by half, skimming fat and residue along the way. Strain through cheesecloth and continue to reduce slowly to about ½ cup.

Chicken Consommé

Yield: 5 cups

1½ quarts Chicken Stock (see recipe above)
6 egg whites
½ cup chopped onion
½ cup chopped celery
½ cup chopped carrot

METHOD Put the stock in a heavy bottomed pan. Whisk egg whites until frothy. Whisk the vegetables into the egg whites, then whisk the mixture into the stock. Heat to a simmer over medium heat, whisking frequently (do not boil). As soon as the stock reaches a simmer, stop whisking, and allow to simmer undisturbed for 45 minutes, so that the egg white *raft* does not break up. Carefully strain through fine cheesecloth. Any type of stock may be clarified using the same procedure.

Juices

Beet Juice

Yield: 1 cup

4 to 5 medium beets
Salt and pepper

METHOD Peel and juice enough beets to make 2 cups of liquid. Slowly reduce by half, skimming away the foam that will result along the way, and season to taste with salt and pepper. The juice can be kept for 3 or 4 days in the refrigerator or it can be frozen.

Bell Pepper Juice

Yield: 1 cup

10 bell peppers, seeded and cut into pieces

METHOD Juice the bell peppers. Slowly reduce the juice by about half, or until it reaches the desired concentration. The juice can be kept 3 or 4 days in the refrigerator or it can be frozen.

Carrot Juice

Yield: 2 cups

12 large carrots

METHOD Peel and juice the carrots. Heat the juice to a simmer over medium-low heat (do not allow to boil, or the juice will become bitter). Skim away the solids as they rise to the top. Continue until the liquid is clear and no more solids rise to the top, about 20 minutes. Strain through a fine cheesecloth. The juice can be kept for 3 or 4 days in the refrigerator or it can be frozen.

Celery Juice

Yield: ½ cup

1 bunch celery

METHOD Juice the celery and pour into a small saucepan. Over medium heat, slowly reduce the celery juice by half, skimming along the way. Strain through a fine cheesecloth. The juice can be kept for 3 or 4 days in the refrigerator or it can be frozen.

Parsley Juice

Yield: ¾ cup

1 bunch parsley (about 2 cups)
⅓ cup ice water
¼ cup grapeseed oil
Salt and pepper

METHOD Blanch the parsley, shock in ice water, and drain. Roughly chop the parsley and place it in a blender with the ice water, grapeseed oil, and salt and pepper to taste. Blend thoroughly and strain through a fine mesh sieve. The juice can be kept for 3 or 4 days in the refrigerator or it can be frozen.

Tomato Coulis

4 cloves garlic, peeled and chopped
2 shallots, peeled and chopped
1 tablespoon olive oil
2 vine-ripened tomatoes, cored and chopped
Salt and pepper

METHOD Sweat the garlic and shallots in olive oil over medium heat until just softened. Add the tomatoes and cook until they are just warmed through, about 2 or 3 minutes. Purée and pass through a fine strainer. Season to taste with salt and pepper. Can be kept for 3 or 4 days in the refrigerator or it can be frozen.

Tomato Water

Yield: 1½ to 2 cups

12 large beefsteak tomatoes
1 tablespoon salt

METHOD Blend the tomatoes and salt in a food processor. Tie up the contents in a cheesecloth and allow the water to drip out. It is best to do this overnight in the refrigerator. The color of the Tomato Water will vary with the type of tomato used and the time of year. Can be kept for 3 or 4 days in the refrigerator or it can be frozen.

Oils, Butters, and Dressings

Herb Oil

Yield: 1 cup

½ cup chives
½ cup parsley
½ cup watercress

½ cup tarragon
2 cups grapeseed oil

METHOD Blanch the herbs in boiling salted water, then immediately shock in cold water and drain. Roughly chop the herbs, squeeze out excess water, and place in the blender with enough oil to cover. Purée until bright green. Add remaining oil, purée for 3 minutes, and pour into a container. Refrigerate for 1 day, strain through a fine mesh sieve, refrigerate 1 more day, and decant.

Saffron Oil

Yield: ¾ cup

1 teaspoon saffron threads
5 tablespoons water
(or less, if a very small pan is used)
⅔ cup grapeseed oil
1½ tablespoons olive oil

METHOD Pan-roast the saffron over low heat for 20 seconds or so to help release the oils present in the spice. Add the water and quickly remove from the heat. Most of the water will immediately steam away. With a rubber spatula, scrape the saffron and any remaining liquid into a blender. Add the oils, blend on high speed for 45 seconds, and allow to sit for 1 day, refrigerated.

Foie Gras Butter

Yield: ⅓ cup

3 tablespoons foie gras
3 tablespoons butter

METHOD Purée in a food processor or blender until smooth. Chill until ready to use.

Red Wine Vinaigrette

Yield: ½ cup

1 small onion, peeled and chopped
12 cloves garlic, peeled and chopped
½ cup plus 2 tablespoons olive oil
1½ cup tomato concassée
4 tablespoons aged balsamic vinegar
2 cups red wine
Salt and pepper

METHOD Sweat the onion and garlic in 2 tablespoons of olive oil until soft and

translucent. Add the tomato and deglaze with the balsamic vinegar. Reduce to a glaze and add the red wine. Reduce by half, strain, and reduce to 3 tablespoons. Whisk in ½ cup of olive oil and season with salt and pepper.

Other Basics

Crispy Pig's Feet

1 whole pig's foot
4 teaspoons grapeseed oil
½ cup chopped onion
½ cup chopped carrot
½ cup chopped celery
3 to 4 cups Chicken Stock (see recipe above)

METHOD In a medium roasting pan, sear the pig's foot on all sides in 2 teaspoons of grapeseed oil. Add the vegetables and continue cooking until they begin to caramelize. Add enough Chicken Stock to cover the pig's foot, cover, and bake at 350 degrees for 2½ hours. Remove the pig's foot from the liquid, debone the meat, and chop into small pieces. Heat 2 teaspoons of grapeseed oil in a small sauté pan over very high heat. Add the meat, cover, and cook for 1½ minutes. Turn the meat over (the pieces will be stuck together) and cook for 1½ minutes. Remove and chop into small pieces again.

Pickled Lamb's Tongues

4 lamb's tongues
⅓ cup peeled and coarsely chopped celery
⅓ cup peeled and coarsely chopped onion
⅓ cup peeled and coarsely chopped carrot
2 cloves garlic
2 tablespoons bacon fat
1 tablespoon grated ginger
12 pieces allspice, lightly pan-roasted
½ cup brown sugar
1 cup rice vinegar
2 cups Chicken Stock (see recipe above)
1 teaspoon salt

METHOD Soak the tongues in repeated changes of cold water for a day or so. In a medium sauté pan, sweat the celery, onion, carrots, and garlic in bacon fat until softened. Add the tongues and brown lightly on all sides for about 15 minutes. Add the remaining ingredients, bring to a boil, and simmer for 2 to 3 hours, or until the meat is very tender. Cool in the liquid. Peel the sheath of skin away from the tongues. The tongues can be served immediately or kept refrigerated for up to 1 week.

Squab Liver Mousse

1 shallot, minced
6 tablespoons butter
12 squab livers
1 tablespoon port wine
½ Granny Smith apple, diced
¼ cup brandy
Salt and pepper

METHOD Sauté the shallots in 2 tablespoons of butter until tender. Remove from the pan and keep warm. Sauté the squab livers in 2 tablespoons of butter until medium-rare, and deglaze with port wine. Sauté the apple pieces in 2 tablespoons of butter until softened, add the brandy, and flame to burn off the alcohol. Place all the ingredients in a food processor, process, and pass through a fine mesh sieve.

Preserved Ginger

Yield: 2 tablespoons

2 tablespoons finely julienned ginger
3 cups cool water
1 cup Simple Syrup (see recipe below)

METHOD Place the ginger in a small saucepan with 1 cup of cool water. Bring to a boil and drain. Repeat this process two more times. Put the drained ginger and Simple Syrup in a small saucepan. Bring to a boil, reduce heat, and allow to simmer for 30 minutes.

Roasted Garlic

2 heads garlic, unpeeled
1½ cups milk (or enough to cover)
1½ cups olive oil (or enough to cover)

METHOD Place the garlic in a small saucepan. Add milk to cover, bring to a boil, and simmer for 10 minutes. Put the garlic in a small ovenproof container, add olive oil to cover, and top with foil. Bake at 250 degrees for 3 hours or until very soft.

Roasted Bell Peppers

4 bell peppers
3 tablespoons olive oil

METHOD Coat the whole bell peppers with olive oil. Place on an open grill and roast until they turn black on one side, about 2 minutes, turn, and repeat. Place the roasted peppers in a bowl, cover with plastic wrap, and let stand for 5 minutes. The skin should then peel off quite easily. Seed the peppers and cut to the desired size.

Simple Syrup

Yield: 1 cup

1 cup sugar
1 cup water

METHOD Combine sugar and water in a small saucepan. Bring to a boil, stirring frequently until all the sugar is dissolved. This will keep indefinitely in the refrigerator.

Cooking Terms, Equipment, and Ingredients

AGAR-AGAR A type of seaweed. Wonderful in broth-based dishes.

BALSAMIC VINEGAR (*aceto balsamico*) A dark, sweet, mellow wine vinegar that is aged in a series of oak and hickory barrels. It is produced only in Modena, Italy. Used primarily as a dressing. The older the vinegar, the sweeter and less acidic it will be. Well-aged balsamic vinegars are available at gourmet food shops.

BATON (*bâtonnet*) A cut the size of a wooden match stick (⅛ x ⅛ x 2 inches).

BRUNOISE Very fine dice approximately ⅛ inch square.

CELLOPHANE NOODLES (bean threads, vermicelli) Clear noodles made from mung beans. They come dried: drop in boiling water for 1 minute. Available in Asian markets.

CHIFFONADE Fine strips, about 1/16 inch wide. Usually used in reference to leafy vegetables, which are rolled up and finely sliced.

CHIOGGA BEETS (or candy cane beets) Very tiny sweet beets with a striped pattern in the flesh.

CONCASSEE See Tomato *Concassée.*

COULIS A very fine purée.

CREME FRAICHE A true crème fraîche is an unpasteurized 30 percent cream that has been allowed to ferment and thicken naturally. It has a nutty, faintly sour flavor. In the United States, crème fraîche is made with whipping cream and buttermilk. Do not substitute with sour cream.

CURRANT TOMATO A very tiny tomato the size of a small currant.

DAIKON A large white Asian radish, relatively mild flavored. Excellent for adding texture and just the right amount of bite.

DEGLAZE When foods have been sautéed or roasted, the coagulated juices are left in the pan. Deglazing is the process of adding liquid to the pan and dissolving these flavorful deposits over heat.

FOIE GRAS Fatted goose or duck liver. All veins must be removed before using.

GELATIN Sheet gelatin is commonly used in Europe; here you may find it at some specialty food shops. If unavailable, substitute 1 teaspoon of gelatin granules for each leaf of sheet gelatin.

GREEN TEA POWDER Used to prepare tea for the Japanese tea ceremony. Can also be used to flavor dessert sauces and syrups.

HIJIKI SEAWEED A rich, chewy, full-flavored seaweed. It cannot be purchased fresh, but dried should be available at most Asian food shops.

HOISIN A thick, sweet, brownish-red sauce made with soybeans, vinegar, sesame seeds, chiles, and garlic. Used in Chinese cooking.

KELP (*kombu, konbu*) A broad-leafed seaweed, commonly used in Japanese cooking for flavoring soups and sauces. Wonderful in broth-based dishes. Usually sold dried or frozen.

LANGOUSTINE A delicate shellfish with very sweet meat that tastes like a cross between lobster and shrimp.

LEMONGRASS A scented grass used as an herb in Southeast Asian cooking. Although the whole stalk may be used, usually the outer leaves are removed and only the bottom third of the stalk is used. Has a lemony-strawlike flavor.

LOVAGE A member of the celery family, with dark green leaves that resemble celery or Italian parsley. An easily grown perennial. The leaves are variously described as tasting of celery, lemons, yeast, pine, and/or basil.

MESCLUN GREENS A mixture of red oak leaf, arugula, frisée, and other small, leafy, buttery, and spicy lettuces.

MIREPOIX A blend of very coarsely chopped onions, carrots, and celery. They are usually sautéed slowly in butter, then added to other preparations.

MIRIN A sweetened rice wine. Used for cooking only.

MISO A fermented soy-bean paste used in Japanese cooking for making soups, sauces, and dressings. Available at most supermarkets.

MONKFISH LIVER A Japanese delicacy that has been referred to as the foie gras of the sea. Special order it from a fish market. Monkfish is also known as angler.

MOULE A food mill.

NOISETTE A circular cut, usually for meat or fish. By extension, a small, round morsel.

OGO (limu ogo) A type of seaweed. Wonderful in broth-based dishes.

PARISIENNE BALL A small round ball about ¼ inch in diameter.

PAVE Any layered preparation cut into a square or rectangle that resembles an old-fashioned paving stone (pavé).

PONZU SAUCE A Japanese dipping sauce made with soy sauce, citrus juice, and rice vinegar. Available bottled.

QUENELLE An oval dumpling made with a forcemeat of fish, veal, or poultry. By extension, the term is also used to mean the typical oval shape. Quenelles can be easily formed with two spoons.

RONDEAU A large, round, heavy-bottomed, ovenproof, medium-deep pot with two loop handles. Good for braising meats.

SALSIFY A root vegetable imported from Belgium. It is available in specialty produce markets. When peeled, the flesh will discolor unless immediately placed in milk or acidulated water.

SHISO (perilla, beefsteak plant) A member of the mint family. Somewhat tangy; tastes like a cross between lemon and mint. Often used as a garnish in Japanese cooking.

SWEAT To cook, uncovered, slowly, over medium or low heat with a very little fat until soft.

TAMARI A dark soy sauce, somewhat thicker and stronger than other soy sauces. It is cultured and fermented like miso. Used in Asian cooking; in Japanese cuisine, used as a dipping or basting sauce.

TERRINE A mold, usually rectangular in shape. Also, the food that has been prepared in the terrine. For recipes in this book, the terrine need not be ovenproof. If you have a terrine that is too large for a given recipe, you can reduce its capacity by taking up the extra space with pieces of raw potato. Line the area to be used with plastic wrap or aluminum foil and proceed with the recipe.

TOMATILLO A small, hard, round fruit that looks and tastes somewhat like a green tomato. May be enclosed in a papery brown husk. Used extensively in Mexican and Southwestern cooking.

TOMATO CONCASSEE Peeled, seeded, and diced tomato.

TRUFFLES A subterranean fungus that is highly prized for its pungent aroma and flavor; found only in certain regions of France and Italy. If fresh truffles are not available, substitute frozen truffles. Scrub thoroughly before using. White truffles are rarer and more expensive than the black. Olive oils that have been infused with the highly pungent white truffle are available in gourmet shops.

TUILE A round wafer that is molded around a curved surface immediately as it comes out of the oven so that it resembles a curved tile (tuile).

WASABI A pungent green Japanese horseradish. Available in paste or powdered form. The powder is mixed with water to produce a smooth sauce.

WATER CHESTNUTS Fresh water chestnuts are so far superior to the canned that you should accept no substitute. Boil for 10 minutes and peel before using. Available in most Asian markets.

Sources

Though it may take a little searching, you can probably find all the ingredients you need right in your own area. For items that are not stocked by your supermarket, check out local ethnic markets and specialty food stores. If that fails, you can contact the suppliers listed below.

Dean and Deluca
560 Broadway
New York, New York 10012
1-800-221-7714
White truffle oil, olive paste, balsamic vinegar.

Star Market, Inc.
3349 North Clark Street
Chicago, Illinois 60657
312-472-0599
Asian dry goods and produce.

Geo. Cornille & Sons Produce
60 South Water Market
Chicago, Illinois 60608
312-226-1015
Fresh produce, seaweed.

Browne Trading Company
260 Commercial Street
Portland, Maine 04101
207-766-2402
Fresh fish and shellfish, monkfish liver.

Wild Game, Inc.
2315 West Huron
Chicago, Illinois 60612
312-278-1661
Foie gras, squab, truffles.

Designed by Adam R. Kallish of Trope: Communication by Design, Chicago

in association with

Michael Glass Design, Inc., Chicago

Color and black and white photography by Tim Turner, Chicago

Black and white photos on

pages 6, 25 right, 46, 116, 130, 144, 157, and 185 are by Scott Trotter

Typeset in Monotype Walbaum by Paul Baker Typography, Inc., Chicago

Printed in Singapore by Tien Wah Press